JESSIE & MICHAEL

Nobody's here. Except Michael and me. But I'm not nervous. I'm petrified!

"It's nice," I tell Michael, commenting on his living room, just for something to say. And to see if my jaw's working.

"Come on," says Michael, holding out his hand for me to take.

"Where?"

He smiles. "My room . . ."

"Uh . . ."

And reaching his hand out to me again, he says, "Come on." *I can't! I can't go through with this!*

Taking his hand, I pull it back, behind my waist—so now his arm is wrapped around me.

"Whatever happens," Michael says, "we go on forever."

"Forever?" I ask him.

"And then some," he nods.

And he leans down and kisses me.

It can't go on like this. Not for long. It has to end—one way or another.

Other Avon Flare Books by
Bruce and Carole Hart

BREAKING UP IS HARD TO DO
CROSS YOUR HEART
SOONER OR LATER

WAITING GAMES

BRUCE AND CAROLE HART

AVON BOOKS  NEW YORK

Cover design: David Kaestle
Cover model: Denise Miller

WAITING GAMES is an original publication of Avon Books. This work has never before appeared in book form.

AVON BOOKS
A division of
The Hearst Corporation
105 Madison Avenue
New York, New York 10016

Copyright © 1981 by The Laughing Willow Company, Inc
Published by arrangement with The Shukat Company, Ltd
Library of Congress Catalog Card Number: 81-65080
ISBN: 0-380-79012-2

Library of Congress Cataloging in Publication Data

Hart, Bruce
  Waiting games
  (An Avon Flare book)
  Summary Fourteen-year-old Jessie becomes romantically and sexually involved with her eighteen-year-old guitar teacher Michael.
    I. Hart, Carole. II. Title.
PZ7.H25628Wai   [Fic]   81-65080
                                                           AACR2

First Avon Flare Printing: November 1981

AVON FLARE TRADEMARK REG. U.S. PAT. OFF. AND IN OTHER COUNTRIES, MARCA REGISTRADA, HECHO EN U.S.A.

Printed in Canada

UNV 30   29   28   27   26   25   24   23

To the cast and crew of *Sooner or Later*,
with deepest respect, affection and gratitude.

One

Sometimes, when I'm alone in my room and it's late at night, after I've turned out the lights and climbed into bed, I switch on the radio and cruise up and down the dial, trying to find something that will shut out the chatter of the day's unanswered questions.

Sometimes, not all that often, but sometimes, cruising up and down the dial, I come across a song—a song I've never heard before, but a song so beautiful, it lifts me out of myself and takes me sailing through its own quiet world.

Almost every time this happens, just before the song comes to an end, just before it returns me to myself—lying in my bed, smiling, on the brink of a long and peaceful sleep—*Gong!*—some raspy-voiced disk jockey smashes a gong and grates out his station's call letters and machine-guns a blare of commercials at me.

It's the pits.

And this—what I'm going through, right now—feels a lot like that.

1

I mean, I *was* listening to a beautiful song I never heard before.

It was called, "I Love Michael and Michael Loves Me and, Even Though He's Seventeen and I'm Not Quite Fourteen, We've Decided—Because We Really Love Each Other—We're Going to Make It Work."

That was the song.

A love song.

It started playing about half an hour ago in the practice room at The Eddie Nova Guitar Institute in Hackensack, where Michael teaches and I take lessons.

It started when Michael forgave me for lying to him about my age and telling him I was sixteen, when I was really thirteen.

Which happened just before Michael opened his arms and took me in and kissed me.

It was a beautiful song, while it lasted.

But it didn't last long enough.

Because, just after Michael and I finished kissing and left the practice room at The Eddie Nova Guitar Institute, and long before the song was over—*Gong!*—all these problems came rushing in on me, roaring inside my head, like blaring commercials.

It's a lot to think about.

Going with a handsome young prince of rock and roll, who just happens to be the sweetest but sexiest man I've ever met, in fact or fiction, is a lot to think about.

Just the difference in our ages.

And our experiences.

Especially with, you know, sex!

But that—like they say—ain't the half of it.

There's also Lois and Bob.

Who just happen to be my mother and father.

They never knew about Michael and me.

Not until this morning.

2

It wasn't until this morning that I told Lois about Michael and me.

I told her everything, too.

About how I went with Michael to a drive-in movie, instead of spending Saturday night with my best friend, Caroline, like I told everybody I was going to.

About how, maybe a third of the way through *Mandingo,* I finally broke down and told Michael I was actually a little more than two years younger than he thought I was.

About how hurt and angry Michael was and how he roared out of the drive-in and how he dropped me off in front of the house and how he roared off down the street and out of my life forever.

I told all that to Lois for the first time, just this morning.

And I gave her my word I'd never go out with Michael again.

And Lois forgave me.

That's the worst part.

She was hurt and angry, too.

But she forgave me.

Right on the spot.

And now, what is she going to say?

What am *I* going to say?

When Michael drops me off at home, about ten minutes from now, how am I going to tell Lois about Michael and me, and how we happen to be—we're—what I guess you'd call—going together?

I mean, Lois is pretty terrific, and so is Bob, but how am I going to get them to understand and approve and support the impossible but beautiful thing that Michael and I are trying to do?

And what if they don't?

And what if they won't?

And what if and what if? And on and on. Etcetera and so forth!

The thing is, like it or not, from where I'm sitting at the moment—which happens to be next to Michael, in the front seat of his old station wagon, tooling down Route 4, heading for my home, in Englewood—it looks like I'm in for nothing but commercials from here on out!

Two

Lois is in the sunroom, upstairs at the back of the house, working in steel wool and kitchen cleanser where she usually works in oils and watercolors.

The sunroom is Lois's studio, her playpen, her refuge.

Whatever quiet moments she can find or make, she spends here, standing at her easel, giving herself over—as she never can in her crowded classroom—to the flow of paint on canvas.

But now—for the first time since longer than she cares to remember—Lois is down on her knees, scrubbing the sunroom floor, scrubbing hard but not too hard, picking up the spatters of paint that come easily, leaving those that come hard.

Cleaned up and waxed over, these mementos of paintings past will stay where they are and, in the hectic times to come, they will serve Lois as a kind of diary, reminding her of the quiet moments that came before and will surely come again.

Not that Lois is expecting hectic times. Today has been hectic enough, thank you.

First, the thing with Jessie this morning.

Lois still blames herself for failing to see the turmoil Jessie must have been going through these last weeks.

Lois has always prided herself on her closeness to her daughter.

But here—without Lois catching so much as a hint of it—Jessie went out on a date, her first date.

And what's more, she went off to a drive-in with a seventeen-year-old boy.

And she never said a word about it.

Not until this morning.

Well, it's over.

As it had to be.

An inexperienced thirteen-year-old like Jessie is no match for a seventeen-year-old—especially a worldly seventeen-year-old like this Michael she went out with undoubtedly is.

And now that this Michael she went out with knows that Jessie is only thirteen and not sixteen, like she pretended she was, he's apparently decided that Jessie is just a kid after all, and a liar in the bargain and—all things considered—not worth his trouble.

"Goodbye and Amen!" Lois tells herself, dipping her steel wool into the water bucket beside her and resuming her scrubbing.

"Mom, I'm home!"

Speak of the devil.

"Up here!" Lois calls, wondering if she's heard something in Jessie's voice, something that might give her a clue to Jessie's mood.

Jessie was pretty shaky when Lois dropped her off at school this morning.

But now, with Jessie pounding up the front stairs, Lois decides she's heard nothing unusual in her voice.

Smiling in anticipation of her daughter's arrival, Lois

6

leaves off her scrubbing, rocks back on her haunches, lifts her eyes to the open doorway and—

"Mom . . . Michael," says Jessie, traipsing into the sunroom, leading a shy but beautiful young man by the hand. "Michael . . . Mom."

"Jesus!" says Lois, gaping up at the beautiful young man.

"Hi," says Michael. "Nice to meet you."

"Michael's my guitar teacher," Jessie explains with a rush. "The one I told you about. He gave me a ride home."

Lois catches her breath, stands, extends her hand to Michael and says, "Thank you."

Not certain she's struck just the right note, Lois watches as Michael's eyes—his blue, blue eyes—travel down her arm to the steel wool she holds, wet and dripping, in her outstretched hand.

"Oh! Excuse me!" she says, embarrassed and juggling the steel wool from hand to hand.

"I just thought you two ought to meet," says Jessie, jumping in to fill the awkward moment.

"Right," says Lois—meaning *"Wrong!"*

"And now that you have," says Jessie, "I guess I'll just see Michael to the door."

"Right," says Lois—meaning *"Right!"*

"Pleasure," says Michael, uncoiling his slow and utterly devastating smile.

"Yes," says Lois—meaning *"Impossible!"*

Taking Michael's hand—*"Like with her father, when she was a toddler,"* Lois thinks—Jessie leads him from the room.

Lois listens to them, the two of them, pounding down the stairs together.

Now Lois looks around the room, as if she might discover someone—anyone—who's seen what she's just seen, heard what she's just heard.

But, of course, there's no one.

7

No one but Lois.

Who—at the moment—is anything but a reliable witness.

"Jesus!" she thinks. "That boy! Boy? Who's kidding who? That 'boy' is a man! A grown man! How can Jessie imagine—?"

"Nice, huh?" says Jessie, suddenly materializing in the doorway.

"Nice?" says Lois, like Jessie's talking some foreign language.

"Yeah," says Jessie, unaware of the invisible language-gap between them. "Isn't he?"

"No," says Lois. "He's not nice. He's gorgeous!"

"Yeah," says Jessie. "A hunk."

"Jessie!"

"I'm sorry," says Jessie, dropping her eyes to the floor.

But then, recovering quickly, Jessie lifts her eyes to meet Lois's eyes. She smiles and continues, "But you have to admit, he is—"

"I thought we had an agreement!" says Lois, interrupting.

Jessie's smile freezes and fades.

"I thought we did, too," she admits.

"We still do!"

"Mom," Jessie begins.

"I don't want to hear about it!"

"Mom!" Jessie protests.

"Not now. Not later. It's over. Finished. Through. Got it?"

"Mom?" Jessie pleads.

Seeing the tears welling in her daughter's eyes, and wishing she could stop them from falling, Lois moves across the room and takes Jessie into her arms.

"I am sorry," says Lois, feeling the tears welling in her own eyes. "Believe me. Please."

Three

Jessie lets the terry robe slip from her shoulders.

Shaking out her auburn hair, she feels it fall—just so—against her milk-white skin.

With one stricken, sea-blue eye she turns and peers over her shoulder into the bathroom mirror, looking to see if she's achieved the effect she's after.

She has.

TEEN ANGEL
HEARTBROKEN
CONDITION CRITICAL
POPE ASKS PRAYERS

Sad and satisfied, Jessie sighs aloud and then—letting her robe slide from her arms and spill from her hips—she steps into the bath. . .

"Aaahh . . ."

9

Relaxing back into the hot, sudsy water, she feels the tension easing, seeping out from every muscle.

"Nothing like a bath," she thinks.

Easing down, slipping deeper, until everything but her chin, her mouth and the tip of her nose is submerged, Jessie welcomes the water, filling her ears, shutting off the world outside.

"Mmmmm . . ."

"Why can't it always be like this?" she wonders.

It's a wish as much as a wonder.

Things have gotten so tense lately.

"Is that the price you have to pay for growing up? Is that why so many grown-ups are so tense?"

"Uhhh . . ."

Rotating her neck, she feels the vertebrae popping, one by one, feels her spine growing limber against the curve of the tub.

"Maybe growing up isn't worth it," she thinks. "Maybe the thing is staying young. And keeping cool. And living laid back. Like Michael."

"Mmmm . . ."

Cupping her breasts in her hands, she thinks of Michael, so strong and yet so gentle.

"Gently, Michael, gently."

Arching her back, she rotates her hips—slowly, slowly—working out the kinks.

"Uhhh . . ."

"Good hips," she thinks, "for bearing children. Which more and more children seem to be doing these days. Not me. I'm not ready for children. Not even Michael's."

"Aaaaahh . . ."

Dipping down from her hips, her stomach runs firm and flat to the curve and slope of her thighs.

"Michael," she thinks, "nothing can keep us apart!"

Four

"It's easy enough to see what the problem is. She's beautiful. My daughter's getting beautiful."

Bob is sitting at the head of the dining-room table.

He's watching Jessie, dishing out salad from the three-legged salad bowl.

He's watching her and remembering.

Lois warned him.

She warned him that one day, the chubby kid in the baggy jeans would turn into a beautiful young woman.

Bob hadn't believed her.

Not until now.

But now that Jessie's appeared upstairs in the sunroom with Young Elvis Presley on her arm, Bob's been forced to take another look at his daughter.

And Lois was right.

She is getting beautiful.

Lois was probably right about not mentioning Jessie and Young Elvis during dinner, too.

Although Lois looked pretty shaken when Bob got

11

home from work, and he would have preferred to get to the bottom of it, right away, before dinner—he'd agreed to hold off.

First, they'd have a nice, quiet dinner.

And then, after dinner, they'd hold a Summit Conference.

That was the agenda for the evening.

It was the way Lois wanted it, and what he'd agreed to.

In matters like this, Bob always deferred to Lois.

Because—he hated to admit it—Lois was closer to Jessie than he was.

She spent more time with Jessie than he did.

She knew more about what was going on with Jessie—inside her—than he did.

Not that Bob and Jessie weren't close. Or that they didn't spend a lot of time together. Or that they didn't talk, and talk about Important Things.

It's just that they rarely got around to talking about Important Personal Things.

Lois got that.

Bob got it from Lois.

So when he got home from work and saw that what he was up against was a Very Important Personal Thing, he'd deferred to Lois.

Not a word about Young Elvis until dinner's over.

"But so far," Bob tells himself, "there hasn't been a word about anything else, either."

The dish-clatter silence is more than he can take.

"Ahem," he says, clearing his throat. "Would anybody like to hear about how I'm doing with the phantom park I'm building around the phantom garage I'm designing for the phantom County Highway Department I'm working for?" he asks hopefully.

"I would," says Lois.

"Really?" he says, surprised.

"But maybe later," Lois admits.

Across the table, Esther—Bob's favorite mother-in-law—asks, "Who has the salt?"

Just loud enough for Lois to hear, Bob mutters, "Ms. Presley."

"Bob!" says Lois.

"Huh?" says Jessie.

Bob smiles his apology at Lois and tells Jessie, "Pass the salt to your grandmother."

"Oh," says Jessie.

And she passes the salt.

"Beautiful," he thinks, watching her. "Lois warned me."

"Mm," says Esther, savoring her salad. "The lettuce!"

"It's hearts," says Lois, accepting her mother's praise with a smile.

"It's Lois's specialty," says Jessie, not looking up from her plate. "Breaking them."

"Jessie!" says Lois, taking the bait.

"Ah-ah!" says Bob, moving to cut it off before it gets started. "This is just the warm-up, Jess. Save your heavy shots for the conference, okay?"

"Conference?" asks Esther.

"Jessie has a . . . a problem, Mom," Lois explains.

"Oh?" says Esther, turning to shower her considerable sympathy on her troubled granddaughter.

"Nothing catastrophic," Lois continues.

"Unless you call life and death catastrophic," Jessie contributes.

"Jessie!" Bob warns her.

"I'll clear the table," says Jessie. "Thanks, Grandma."

Rising from the table, Jessie begins gathering the dishes.

As she does, she tells herself that Esther's sympathy—as sweet as it is—won't do her any good now. She doesn't need sympathy now. If she's going to work

13

this thing out—and she *is* going to—what she needs is courage. She has to be strong.

"I'm reading a very good book," says Esther to no one in particular. "By Norman Mailer. *The Executioner's Song,* it's called.

"I think," says Esther, continuing as she rises from her chair, "I think I will read in my room. So I won't be interrupted."

"Good night, Esther," says Bob, rising from his chair to kiss her.

"Good night," says Esther pleasantly.

But she walks right past Bob and continues out the door.

Five

The Summit Conference is now in session.

Sitting in his wing chair, adjacent to the couch, Bob holds a match over the bowl of his pipe. He pulls and he puffs, sending up clouds of smoke, until—at last—he achieves lift-off.

"So," he says, turning to his wife and his daughter, who are seated a comfortable distance apart from each other on the couch across from him. "Any old business?"

"Bob!" says Lois—obviously uncomfortable and anxious to have the unhappy business aired and over with.

"I just want to make it clear that we're all friends, here," Bob explains. "In addition to being close relatives and occasional opponents, we're all friends."

"I don't think there's any question about that," says Lois.

Turning to her daughter, she asks, "Is there, Jessie?"
Jessie has to admit there isn't.

15

Although, in her position, it's hard to admit anything.

Because once you admit one thing, admitting the next thing is easier, and so you're liable to just go on admitting one thing after another, until—before you know it—you've lost the whole argument.

Still, there's no question about all of them being friends.

And so Jessie admits it.

"But that doesn't mean you're always right about what's right for me," she insists.

"A good point," says Bob. "Which is why we're all here, talking about what's right for you."

"Michael's right for me," she says.

He nods his head.

"Convince me," he says. "Convince your mother."

"I don't know if you'll listen," says Jessie.

She looks from Bob to Lois.

"We'll listen," Lois assures her.

"Okay," says Jessie.

She takes a deep breath.

She lets it out real slow.

She thinks, *"Here goes!"*

She says, "I love Michael."

"Oh?" says Bob.

He looks surprised. And, finally, dead serious. But unfortunately, not convinced.

"And he loves me," Jessie continues.

"Uh-huh," says Bob, nodding his head, taking it in.

"And he knows how old I am," says Jessie.

"Now," adds Lois.

"Since you told him," says Bob. "Last Saturday night, wasn't it?"

Jessie takes another deep breath and bites the bullet.

"I'm sorry about that," she says.

"So your mother tells me," Bob answers.

"I'm telling you," says Jessie, "I'm really sorry I lied and went behind your back and . . . It was a rotten

16

thing to do. To both of you. I know it. And I'm sorry. I'm very sorry. Honest."

"Well," says Bob, letting her off the hook. "It's okay. Everybody does something rotten once in a while. Even me. I know you won't believe it, but just ask your mother."

"Scout's Honor," says Lois, giving Jessie her smile and holding up two spread-apart fingers in the mistaken belief that the Scout Salute and the Peace Sign are one and the same.

"Please, Lois," Jessie thinks. "Please, don't be irresistible."

"He's seventeen," says Bob, picking up the conversation.

"He's very sweet," Jessie replies.

"He's gorgeous!" Lois charges.

"You hold that against him?" asks Jessie.

"I wouldn't **dare** hold anything against him!" Lois counters.

"Ooooo!" says Bob, impressed and scoring one for Lois.

But Lois declines the point.

"I'm sorry," she tells Jessie. "I don't hold his good looks against him. I don't. Really. It's just that . . . Well . . . Don't you think he may be just a little too much for you to handle, Jessie?"

"Four years is a big difference at your age," says Bob, stating the obvious—the painfully obvious.

Jessie can't deny it.

"I know it," she admits. "And so does Michael. We've talked about it."

"Good," says Bob.

"How did it go?" asks Lois.

"Word for word?" asks Jessie.

"Of course not," Lois answers.

"We'd just like to know," says Bob, stumbling. "How do you two plan to . . . uh . . . *handle* things."

Jessie can't believe her ears.

17

Neither can Lois.

They look at each other.

And burst out laughing.

For a moment, Bob looks bewildered, but—playing back the tape in his head—he finally hears what he's said.

"So?" he says, defending himself from their laughter. "Everybody's not Shakespeare. Even Shakespeare wasn't Shakespeare. So why should I be?"

"Seriously, Jessie," says Lois, regaining her composure and taking her daughter's hand.

It takes Jessie a moment to sober up.

But then she's stone sober.

"Michael's going to follow my lead," she says. "He's going to let me set the pace."

"The pace of what?" Lois snaps.

As if she didn't know.

"You know," Jessie answers.

"No, I don't," says Lois. "Unless you mean love-making. And if that's what you mean, I'll tell you the pace you'll set. Stop! Dead stop!"

There it is.

Out in the open.

The stone wall Jessie's been up against all along.

Jessie tells herself she should have known, and then—angry and challenging—she says, "Oh, fine!"

Rising to the challenge, Lois begins, "Don't you—!"

"Whoa!" shouts Bob. "Slow down! We're all friends here. Remember?"

"I'm sorry," says Lois. "I just get upset when I think about our thirteen-year-old daughter setting the pace for—"

"He agreed to this arrangement? . . . Michael?" asks Bob.

"He promised," says Jessie.

Bob laughs softly and shakes his head.

"It isn't that long since I was a young man," he tells her. "I remember it pretty well. I remember what it was like being a young man. Being a young man with a beautiful girl. I made promises, too.

"I don't think it will work, Jess. I don't think you should see him anymore."

"Mom!"

"I'm sorry, Jessie," says Lois.

"You can't!" Jessie cries. "You can't stop me from seeing him!"

She's on her feet now and glaring down at Bob, still seated in his chair.

His eyes meet hers.

"Yes," he tells her. "I can."

"How?" she demands, almost shouting. "How can you stop me?"

"By reminding you," he tells her, speaking slowly, fighting hard to control his rising temper. "By reminding you that I am your father. . . . And Lois is your mother. . . . And you are our daughter. . . . And by telling you that Lois and I, your father and mother, forbid it! We forbid you to see Michael! . . . Do you understand? . . . Jessie? . . . Do you?"

"You can't!"

She shouts it.

She runs across the room, shouting it.

"You can't! You can't!"

Sobbing, she reaches the hallway and, racing up the stairs two and three at a time, she shouts it.

"You can't! You can't! You can't!"

Reaching the top of the stairs, she runs across the second-floor landing to her room.

Downstairs, Bob and Lois sit silently, listening to the slam of Jessie's door and the muffled sobs that follow in its wake.

"What are we going to do?" asks Lois.

Bob heaves a heavy sigh.

"I'm going to have a beer," he says.

Lois nods her head.

"I guess I'll see what's on television," she says.

19

As she stands and moves toward the stairs, Bob bends over the ashtray and begins emptying his pipe. Over his shoulder, he asks her, "Is he really gorgeous?"

Pausing at the foot of the stairs, Lois turns to him and answers, "A hunk."

As she begins climbing the stairs, Bob nods his head and then, to himself, he says, "Wonderful."

Now, his pipe emptied, he rises from his chair and begins turning out the lights.

The Summit Conference stands adjourned.

Six

Michael, Michael . . .
I won't give you up . . .
Why should I?
Because you're beautiful?
Because you're kind?
What kind of reason is that?
Seventeen is a number!
Seventeen minus thirteen and eleven-twelfths equals
three and one-twelfth.
You're thirty-seven twelfths older than me.
So what?
If I love you . . .
If you love me . . .
What's the difference?
Thirty-seven twelfths?
Shoo!
They're gone!
Blown away.
Nothing at all.

Twelfths . . .
"Jessie!"
It's Lois.
Calling me.
What time is it?
Must be three in the morning.
Three . . .
"Jessie?"
Her voice is closer now.
Softer.
She opens the door.
"It's him," she says.
"What's him?" I ask her.
"The phone," she says.

She's standing in the doorway. Dressed for bed. She has something to say. Advice to offer. But she doesn't offer it.

She nods her head. And closes the door. And departs.

"Michael!"

I roll across my bed, reach down to the floor and lift the phone to my ear.

"Michael?"

"Yeah."

"What time is it?"

"Uh . . ." he says, looking somewhere for the time.

"Wait a minute!" he says, catching himself. "Is that the way you say hello?"

"I'm sorry," I confess.

"It's okay," he says, forgiving me completely.

"Hello, Michael."

"Hi, Jess," he smiles.

I can feel it through the wires.

"It's a little after ten," he says.

"What is?" I ask him.

"The time!" he laughs.

"Oh," I tell him, still lost in his smile. "It is?"

"You been drinking?" he asks.

22

"Michael!"

"Well," he says, "you sound pretty weird."

"I fell asleep," I explain.

"Rough day, huh?"

It's a joke. But I don't laugh. I change the subject.

"Terrific day," I tell him.

"Yeah," he says. "Me, too."

"Michael . . . ?"

"Yeah?"

"Are we going to be able to do this?"

"You mean talk on the phone?" he asks.

"Michael!"

"Yeah," he says. "I think we can handle it."

"Michael!"

He laughs.

"Jess," he says, "I love you, and there's nothing we can't do."

He believes it.

I want to believe it, too.

"You really think so?" I ask him.

"I know so," he says. "Don't you?"

"I do now," I tell him.

"Well," he says, "try to keep it in mind. Okay?"

"Okay," I tell him, smiling and hoping he can feel it through the wires, the way I can.

"Why I called," he says, "is Saturday. Saturday night."

"Yes," I tell him, accepting right-off-the-bat whatever offer he's about to make.

"Wait a minute!" he laughs. "Not so fast!"

"I thought *I* set the pace," I tell him.

It's a joke. But he doesn't laugh. He sounds like he's blushing.

"Uh . . ." he says. "Right. . . . Anyway . . ."

"Saturday," I remind him.

"Yeah," he says. "Right. Saturday night. Wow! I'm getting as weird as you are!"

"Never!" I tell him.

23

He breaks up.

"Probably not," he admits.

"Saturday."

We both say it together.

And break up.

"We're playing at this place called The County Line," he says. "You heard of it?"

"No," I confess.

"Yeah," he laughs. "It's that kind of place . . . but anyway, would you like to come along?"

I close my eyes.

An instant prayer.

One word.

One . . .

I tell him, "Sure!"

Seven

Sure, is exactly what I'm not.

From the moment my conversation with Michael comes to an end, I swim (and sink) and sink (and swim) in a sea of indecision.

"I don't want to lie to them," I tell myself.

Lying to my parents—lying to them again—telling them I'm not going out with Michael when, in fact, I'm going no place else but out with Michael—well, that's something I could do. And God knows, it's something I've done. But it's also something I never want to do again!

I mean, what good does it do? Pretending I'm not doing what I am doing? Pretending I'm not who I am?

After a while, won't I just become an expert at what I didn't? And who I'm not?

And when it comes down to who I am—and what I stand for—and what I won't stand for—won't I just wind up a Total Airhead?

"Why get into a thing like that?" I ask myself.

I've been lying across the bed all this time, right where Michael left me.

But now I roll over on my back and begin unbuttoning my blouse.

I've reached a decision.

I unsnap my jeans and sigh with relief.

I will not lie to my parents about my date with Michael.

Unless I absolutely have to.

Eight

"I owe it to them. I owe it to my parents to tell them the truth."

It's Tuesday morning, and I'm sitting in biology lab, dissecting an illustrated frog with the eraser at the end of my pencil.

I could have had a real frog if I wanted one, and a real scalpel.

But I cast my lot with the Squeamish Wing of the Humane Society, and wound up with *The Optional Illustrated Frog Book* and the eraser at the end of my Eberhard Faber.

"Slicing into" the illustrated epidermis of my illustrated frog, I find myself imagining how it's going to be, now that there's no turning back.

"Bob. Lois. I'm going out with Michael. Saturday night. No matter what. Whether you approve or not. Because. Well. Because what's the point of being in love if you can't go out on Saturday night with the man that you're in love with? None. You see?"

It will probably go something like that.

I shudder at the thought.

But now that I've "sliced into" my illustrated frog, it's time to move on.

I turn the page of my fake frog book and—*Zap!*—a rainbow of illustrated frog innards punches me right in the eye.

"Yech!"

Quickly, I turn back to the first page of *The Optional Illustrated Frog Book*. My fake frog looks a lot better wearing his Kermit suit.

"I owe my parents a chance," I think. *"A chance to hear what I've decided to do. A chance to disagree with my decision. A chance to disapprove of my decision.*

"I owe them a chance—for the very last time—to forbid my going out with Michael.

"And then—when I insist on going through with my decision, when I go walking out the door and into the night with Michael—I owe them a chance to yell at me and threaten me.

"I owe them a chance to run upstairs and pack up my things and leave my suitcase on the front porch—waiting for me when I get home.

"They've left a note, scotch-taped to the handle of the suitcase.

"Lightning cracks the midnight sky. A driving rain comes pelting down. I turn up the collar of my coat. I rip open the envelope and read—

Dear Jessie,
   As far as we're concerned, from now on, you are dead.

                Good luck,
                Mom and Dad

"I crumple the note in my hand, stuff it in my trenchcoat pocket, lift my suitcase and—never looking

back—I trudge out into the rain, out into the heart of the night. . . . Another Victim of Telling the Truth!"

"Problem?" says Mr. Demerino.

He's standing right beside me, looking down at page one of my fake-frog book.

"Rubber scalpel," I explain, showing him my eraser.

"Get busy!" he says, and he turns and marches off, searching the room for signs of other dirty-rotten, chicken-hearted frog lovers like me.

Gritting my teeth—*"Sorry, Kermit"*—I drive the dagger deep into his chest.

Nine

To lie or not to lie.

That is the question.

By Tuesday afternoon, I've got myself so confused, I'm ready to turn almost anywhere for advice. So—

Sitting on the crowded bus that takes me home from school, I turn to my best friend—Caroline.

Even though Caroline is still at the stage where she dreams more about kisses made of chocolate than kisses made of mouths, I trust her—if not for giving useful advice, at least for keeping secrets. So—

Sitting on the bus—its aisles packed with rowdy kids just let out of school—I turn to Caroline.

"What would you think—?" I begin.

"Cut it out!" Caroline barks.

My eyes go wide.

My jaw drops like a stone.

I can't believe it.

Caroline—sweet Caroline—never barks.

At anyone.

Never!

It isn't until I follow the direction of Caroline's icy stare that I realize her outburst wasn't meant for me.

Caroline's bark was directed at this Big Guy, standing in the aisle.

This Big Guy, standing over us.

This Big Guy, who's just standing there with his buddies, staring right back at Caroline.

Staring right back at her and smiling.

Smiling and whistling.

Just whistling away.

"Cut it out!" Caroline barks again—and this time, you can almost see the spiky icicles flying from her eyes.

But this Big Guy, he just starts laughing and he turns to his buddies and he says, "See? I told ya!"

And then they all start laughing.

"So awful!" Caroline hisses through clenched teeth. In her lap, her hands are balled into fists.

"What?" I ask her.

"Them!"

"What were they laughing about?"

"That song!"

"The song he was whistling?" I ask her. "What was it?"

Muttering through her clenched jaw, Caroline answers, "'Nothin' Could Be Finer Than To Be In Carolina In the Morning'!"

I know I shouldn't.

But I can't help myself.

I start laughing.

Caroline glares at me.

"I'm sorry," I tell her. "Really."

31

But I can't stop myself.

Furious, Caroline twists around in her seat and glares out the window.

Still struggling to control my laughter, I decide to postpone this afternoon's edition of "Ask Caroline!"

I make a mental note: *"Consult local listings for date and time of rescheduling."*

Ten

That night, Michael calls.

He tells me about The Skye Band and the rehearsal they had this afternoon to get themselves ready for their Saturday gig at The County Line.

I tell Michael about Caroline and the Big Guy on the bus.

Which makes him laugh.

Which makes me nervous. And leaves me wondering why I brought it up in the first place.

But Michael changes the subject.

He wants to talk about who calls who.

He'd like it if I called him sometimes.

Just so I won't seem too obvious, I take a minute and "consider."

Then I tell him, "Sure."

There's that word again!

"Great!" says Michael.

And he gives me his phone number.

And I pretend to write it down.

Because I've had Michael's number written in my phone book for about a month now.

In fact, I got it from the Information Operator the same day that Michael first mentioned where he lived.

At the time, just writing Michael's number in my phone book made me feel I knew him a lot better than I actually did.

And somehow, just having Michael's number written in my phone book made it seem more likely that someday, I would know Michael better.

Not that I believe in magic, but—with Michael on the other end of the line, giving me the number I've already got—I don't exactly *not* believe in magic, either.

So anyway, after I pretend to write Michael's number in my book, he tells me I should feel free to call him, any time.

And I tell him I will.

And he tells me he's glad.

And then, after a little bit more, Michael says he's sorry, but it's getting late and he still has to hit his books.

So I tell him I'm sorry, too, and I say good night and he says, "See you Saturday."

"Friday," I tell him.

I have my regular guitar lesson with Michael after school on Friday.

"Right," says Michael. "See you Friday *and* Saturday."

"Sure," I say.

And I sigh.

And I say, "Well . . ."

And he says, "Well . . ."

And I say, "Good night."

And he says, "'Night, Jess."

34

Eleven

It's Wednesday.

After school, I get off the bus at the stop before the one I usually get off at.

I need some time to myself, and stretching out the walk home seems like a good way to get it.

The thing is, time is getting short, and I still haven't made up my mind about what to do.

To lie or not to lie?

That is still the question.

"A question for a daisy," I tell myself.

Maybe it's because I'm walking past my old, boarded-up grammar school and—among the weeds that overgrow its front lawn—I've spotted sprays of wild daisies.

Or maybe it's Fate.

I pick a daisy and begin the count-down.

"Lie to them," I think, pulling the first petal from the daisy.

"Tell them the truth," I think, pulling the second petal.

"This is stupid," I think.

I apologize.

"Sorry, daisy."

But just so the daisy won't have died in vain, I invent a brand-new superstition, right on the spot.

Tossing the daisy with the two plucked petals over my left shoulder, I make a wish.

"I wish it was two years from now, and Michael and The Skye Band and me were just finishing up our first world tour with a final concert at Madison Square Garden. And Bob and Lois are coming to see us—all smiling and happy and proud—in the limousine we've sent for them."

"Hey, everybody!"

Michael's at the microphone.

The Garden—filled to overflowing—is in a frenzy.

"Something I want to say!" he shouts.

And—just like that—the roar of the crowd drops down to a murmur.

"None of this could have happened," he says, "without the love of my woman."

The crowd erupts in cheers and whistles as the spotlight runs across the stage and comes to rest on the beaming young woman with the auburn hair and the brimming blue eyes.

"And none of it could have happened," he shouts, "without the understanding of her folks. . . . Bob! . . . Lois! . . . Stand up!"

A little embarrassed, Bob and Lois rise from their seats in the front row.

As the crowd roars its gratitude, they throw kisses to the happy couple at the center of the stage.

And now, turning, Bob and Lois throw their kisses to the roaring crowd.

But it isn't two years later.

It isn't Show Time at Madison Square Garden.

As a matter of fact, it's Dinner Time on Twining Court, in Englewood, New Jersey.

And everybody's edgy.

Trying to sound casual—but sounding like she's trying to sound casual—Lois asks me if I've got anything planned for the weekend.

"Uh . . ." I answer—sounding no more casual than she does. "Not so far."

"Sounds like fun!" says Bob, taking a stab at humor.

I give him a smile for his trouble.

At least I have the consolation of knowing I haven't told a lie.

I don't have anything planned for the weekend.

Not so far, anyway.

Because I haven't made up my mind yet.

Because I can't make up my mind.

I've got to call Michael.

"Houdini," says Esther.

"Gesundheit!" says Bob.

"Who?" says Lois.

"Houdini!" Esther corrects her. "Gary Gilmore was related to Houdini."

"Oh," says Lois.

"How about that?" says Bob.

"Yeah," I say.

Twelve

After dinner, alone in my room, with my radio playing
to cover the sound, I dial Michael's number.
  I wait while the phone rings.
  Once.
  Twice.
  Three times.
  How big is his house?
  Maybe he's taking a shower.
  You'd think somebody'd be home.
  Eight.
  Is enough.
  Click!
  I hang up.
  And feel the tears starting in my eyes.
  I know where Michael is.
  Out with another girl.
  Another woman.
  "Oh, Michael! I've lost you!"
  Throwing myself onto my bed, I bury my head in my
pillow and cry myself to sleep.

Thirteen

Good afternoon, America! And welcome to the fabulous "Lunch Room," deep in the heart of fabulous J.F.K. Junior High, where it's Thursday and it's time for . . . "Ask Caroline!"

You wouldn't know it to look at it—it looks like feeding time at the zoo—but the school cafeteria turns out to be the perfect place for swapping the deepest, darkest secrets.

It's because of how noisy it is.

With the dishes banging and everybody shouting over the rock music the student government's got piped in for lunch hour, you can say anything to anybody and never think twice about being overheard.

So I tell Caroline about how I've made this date with Michael for Saturday night.

And how I can't decide whether or not I should tell my parents about it.

And how I've been thinking I might be better off just breaking the date, although breaking a date with Michael would be like breaking my own heart.

39

And how just trying to decide what to do is driving me crazy.

And Caroline just sits there through the whole thing, saying nothing, looking beautiful and bewildered—like some fairy-tale princess from outer space who's just come face to face with her first *Kiss* concert.

Even so, I take the plunge.

"What would you recommend?" I ask her.

"How should I know?" she shrugs.

"I don't expect you to know," I tell her. "I just want your opinion."

"Oh," says Caroline. "Let me think about it."

"Sure," I tell her. "Until when?"

"How's Sunday?" she asks, trying to slip it by me.

"Fair and warmer," I tell her.

"Okay," she sighs. "After school."

"Thanks," I tell her.

I make a mental note—"*'Ask Caroline!' the program usually seen at this time, has been rescheduled for airing immediately after school today, so that we could bring you the following* 'Blue-Plate Special!'"

Closing my eyes, I dig my fork into the mystery meat that's cowering under the congealed gravy on my lunch tray.

When it fails to cry out, I open my eyes and dig in.

Yum!

Salisbury steak!

Pass the ketchup!

Fourteen

After school, Caroline and I hop the bus into Hackensack and head for The Station—which is this ice cream and soda shop they've put inside this old abandoned railroad station.

If you're going to The Station—where everybody always goes—you don't go there directly.

You have to spend a little time wandering around, pretending you're not going there, so—when you do wind up there—it isn't like you planned it.

It's more like you were just passing by and happened to drop in.

It's cooler that way. And Caroline and I are very cool.

Which is why we happen to be lugging our overstuffed book bags down Pearl Street at the moment.

If my sense of direction is any good, Pearl Street should bring us out about a block down from The Station. A perfect place to drop in from.

And then when we get to The Station, Caroline will

give me all the advice I'm desperate enough to ask her for.

But meanwhile, we're *schlepping* along Pearl Street, talking about this and that and mostly nothing at all. Except, now—like it was just part of the general chatter we've got going—Caroline says, "So what have you decided to do about Michael?"

Which stops me dead in my tracks.

"Oh, no," I tell her. "You promised me you'd give me your advice."

For a second, Caroline looks embarrassed.

But then, she drops her eyes and kind of slumps her shoulders, and what she looks like is very sad.

"I'm sorry," I tell her, apologizing for whatever it is I've done to make her look so sad.

"No," she says, still not looking at me. "It isn't you."

Now it's me who's embarrassed.

Sometimes, when you get all wrapped up in your own problems, you forget that other people—like, for example, your own best friend—they have their problems, too.

I walk over close to Caroline and, real softly, I ask her, "What's wrong?"

She lifts her eyes, and I can see, by the set of her jaw, she's not sad anymore. She's angry.

"How am I supposed to give you advice," she wants to know, "when I don't know anything about it?"

And now Caroline looks like she's going to start bawling. Right here. In broad daylight. In the middle of Pearl Street.

"Hey, Caroline," I tell her.

"Aren't you scared?" she shouts.

Shouts!

"Shhh," I say, trying to calm her down before we start drawing a crowd.

And, really calm and quiet, I ask her, "Scared of what, Caroline?"

42

"You know," she says, accusing me—like I've betrayed her, or something.

"No," I tell her. "Honestly. I don't."

"Sex!" she shouts.

Shouts!

"Caroline!" I tell her. "Keep it down, will you?"

"He's seventeen!" she says.

"I know," I sigh.

She's got me thinking about it now.

"Well?" she says.

"Yeah," I tell her. "I'm scared."

"You are?" she beams.

I mean, I can see the clouds lifting off her.

It breaks me up!

"Yeah," I tell her. "Of course I am."

"You mean you haven't—?" she asks me.

"Caroline!" I say—like "How dare you!" and "Of course not!" at the same time.

"Oh, Jess," she says, throwing her arms around me—right here, in broad daylight, in the middle of Pearl Street!

But who cares?

"I want us always to be friends," she says.

"Best friends," I tell her.

"Yeah," she says, releasing me and stepping back.

"You don't have to worry about me," I assure her.

"I know," she says. "And anyway, one of us has to go first."

"Unless we don't go at all," I tell her.

She looks at me.

I look at her.

We both know that's not the way it's going to be.

And so we laugh.

And that, thank goodness, is that.

We start walking down Pearl Street again.

For a while, neither of us says anything. We just walk.

After a while, though, I start rummaging around in my head, looking for another subject to bring up.

But I can't come up with anything.

So what I do is, while we're walking along, I look over at Caroline and, real casually, I ask her, "You got any more advice to give me?"

Caroline looks over at me and laughs, and then she says, "No, but I bet *she* does!"

I look where Caroline's pointing, across Pearl Street to this abandoned storefront.

In the window of this abandoned storefront, there's a homemade sign that says—

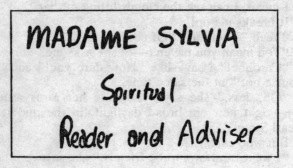

"Wow!"

I can't believe it!

But Caroline—even though it's her own discovery—isn't all that impressed. It's The Station she's interested in.

"Come on," she says.

The thing is, Caroline doesn't recognize Fate when she sees it.

You have to lead her to it, step by step.

"Have you ever seen that store before?" I ask her.

"I don't usually walk on Pearl Street," Caroline answers.

"Exactly!" I tell her. "Neither do I!"

"So?" says Caroline.

She doesn't get it.

"Look," I tell her, "I've got three dollars. Minus the bus home."

"What about The Station?"

"I'll pay you back," I promise.

"I know you'll pay me back," she tells me.

She's thoroughly exasperated with me.

But even so, Caroline lifts her book bag from her shoulder and drops it to the sidewalk and kneels down and starts fishing through it, looking for her wallet.

"Eight dollars," she says, "minus fifty cents."

"We've got ten dollars," I tell her.

"It won't be enough," she says.

"Come on," I tell her.

And before she can answer, I'm on my way across the street, heading for my Appointment with Destiny.

Fifteen

The little bell above the door tinkles as we enter Madame Sylvia's abandoned storefront.

Inside, it's like an empty grocery store with deep shelves all around the walls.

Except now, the old grocery store has been turned into a kind of living room with a rug and lots of old but nice furniture—like Grandma had at her house when Grandpa was still alive.

It's kind of quiet and cozy.

Except for the two big display windows that look right out into the street.

"Nobody's here," says Caroline.

"Hello," I call.

"Oh!" says this funny, piping voice. "We've got company!"

"Yoo-hoo!" the voice pipes—it's coming through a doorway that leads to the back of the store. "We're on our way. Make yourselves at home, girls."

"How did she know?" I wonder.

Caroline wonders, too. I can see by the look on her face.

"Here we are!" says Madame Sylvia, entering from the back room.

"Meow!" says the black cat she has draped across her shoulders.

"Now, behave, Elmo!" she tells the cat.

"Always speaking when he hasn't been spoken to," she explains.

"Don't be boisterous, Elmo," she warns the cat.

"Shall we, then?" she says, motioning us over to a round table on the other side of the room.

And—not waiting for an answer—she turns and totters off toward the table.

Madame Sylvia is pretty old and shaped like a barrel with two spindly legs.

She's wearing a pretty old dress, too, one that comes down almost to her ankles.

But Madame Sylvia's eyes are young, and her face is kind, and her hair—which is probably really gray or even white—is bright red with henna and piled on top of her head in an elaborate hairdo that she's got held together with a whole collection of tortoise-shell combs.

As Madame Sylvia totters toward the table, I look over at Caroline and motion her to follow me.

But Caroline just shakes her head and perches herself on the arm of an overstuffed chair, right near the door. Caroline is not what you'd call "adventurous."

I turn around and walk over to the round table and I sit down across from Madame Sylvia.

"Is this your first time, then?" she asks me.

"Uh . . . yes," I admit.

"I'm Sylvia."

"Oh," I say, "Jessie. Jessie Walters. How do you do? This is—"

47

"Caroline," says Caroline, from her perch near the door.

Madame Sylvia smiles across the room to Caroline and then she turns back to me.

"It's ten dollars, dear. Payable in advance."

"Caroline?" I say, turning to look over at her.

Reluctantly, Caroline rises from her perch and walks across the room and hands her seven dollars to me.

I tell her thanks and, adding my three dollars to her seven, I pass it across the table to Madame Sylvia.

"You can sit, dear," Madame Sylvia tells Caroline, nodding to an empty chair.

"Might as well have a peek at what you're paying for," she says.

Caroline looks at me.

She is not happy.

But she sits.

And Madame Sylvia smiles.

And she reaches out and lifts a fat deck of oversized cards from the table.

"The Tarot," she says.

"I do other bits," she explains. "Palms and crystals and tea leaves and the like. But the Tarot's best where love's concerned."

Caroline and I look at each other.

How did she know?

Madame Sylvia laughs.

"Did I guess right?" she asks.

"Yes," I tell her.

"I knew we'd hit it off," says Madame Sylvia, riffling the big deck of cards. "You're an only child?"

Speechless, I nod my head.

"A Hebrew?" Madame Sylvia asks. "If you don't mind my asking."

"Yes."

Madame Sylvia smiles and nods her head.

"Very psychic, Hebrews. All that time in Egypt, I

48

expect. That's where the Tarot is from. Here," she says, handing me the cards. "Shuffle them, dear."

She hands me the cards with their faces up. As I shuffle them, I can see the pictures on the cards—pictures of Kings and Queens and cups and castles and moons and chariots and swords and a man, hung upside down, and the Devil and Death.

But now, Madame Sylvia tells me to turn the cards over and keep on shuffling them until I feel like they're well mixed.

Then, when I feel the cards are well mixed, Madame Sylvia tells me to divide them into six stacks, with seven cards in each one.

And then, as I follow the rest of Madame Sylvia's instructions, she explains how the Tarot is as old as the Pyramids and the Sphinx, and how the Knowledge of the Tarot passed out of Egypt in the hands of Gypsies, who wandered the whole world over—right down to our own time—preserving and perfecting the Wisdom of the Tarot.

"Where did you get it from?" asks Caroline—like she's the arresting officer and Madame Sylvia is the suspect.

But Madame Sylvia just smiles and takes it in stride.

"From a Gypsy," she says. "Back home. Many years ago."

By now—following Madame Sylvia's instructions—I've got the cards spread out on the table, with the weird pictures arranged in six neat rows of seven cards each.

To me, the whole tabletop looks like a page of comic strips torn out of the Sunday Supplement of an ancient Egyptian newspaper. Except—probably because I haven't hung out with that many Gypsies—the cartoons don't make all that much sense to me.

But they do to Madame Sylvia.

They make a lot of sense.

For instance—just by looking at the cards—Madame Sylvia can tell me that I've had "a happy, although relatively short Past."

And that my mother is "artistically inclined."

And that my father's "some sort of builder or architect or some such."

And quite a bit more.

Like about my grandfather dying.

And how Caroline and me have been "best chums" since the first time we met.

Madame Sylvia also sees my "stormy Present" in the cards.

She can see how I'm being "pushed and pulled, hither and fro" because of the different loyalties I feel "toward Mum and Dad, and to your beau, and to yourself, too.

"Very loyal to yourself," she says. "Your first loyalty. And that's a good sign, too. Even if, every now and again, it does get you in rather deep waters.

"But let's don't dwell on it," she says. "The Future's the thing. Let's see . . ."

And, studying the cards, she begins reading my Future.

"Well!" she says. "There you are. Gone off on your own again. And never mind Mum and Dad. I can see your young man all through here."

"You can?" I ask her.

"Oh, yes!" she says. "Plain as day. Not that I blame you. He is something, isn't he?"

"Yes," I tell her.

"Very good-looking? Exceptional-looking?" she asks.

"Yes!" Caroline gasps.

Madame Sylvia looks at Caroline, smiles and looks back at the cards on the table.

Tapping her finger on one card, she warns me, "Vanity could be a problem. It often is with exceptional-looking young men."

I look at the card she's tapping on but I don't see vanity.

"It doesn't mean it *has* to be a problem," she says. "It's just something to be looked out for—to be on guard against, you see."

"Uh-huh," I tell her.

"Are we happy in the Future—Michael and me?"

"Very," she says. "At least, for a time."

"Not forever?" I ask her.

"Oh," she laughs. "I can't tell you that. That's up to you. The Tarot only tells us about Conditions. It's up to us to make our own Fate, within the Conditions it describes."

"Oh."

"But all in all," she says, collecting the cards from the table, "when we choose to follow our own paths, and not the paths others might like us to follow, we have to be prepared to enjoy the rare pleasures we encounter, just as we steel ourselves to the pain that comes with living our own lives.

"That's not an easy thing to learn. But at least you'll never regret living by the lights of others. And you'll never regret not living at all.

"Lots of people do, you know. But—for good or ill—you're not one of them.

"Do you see?"

"Yes," I tell her.

And—Heaven help me—I do see.

I see now what it is I have to do.

Sixteen

Friday morning.

As I get ready to leave my room—heading for the kitchen, and then the bus, and then to school—I grab my guitar.

It's all packed up in its black cardboard case, leaning in the corner, where I always keep it.

Grabbing my guitar as I head out of my room on Friday mornings is a habit I've taught myself since I first started taking guitar lessons.

I don't even think about it anymore.

Except now, feeling the weight of the guitar in my hand, I think, *"Michael!"*

When I promised Lois and Bob I'd never go out with Michael again—a promise I haven't broken, yet—did they think I meant I'd never *see* him again?

Like at guitar lessons?

Oh, God!

Of course they did!

But that's not what I meant.

I didn't.

Terrific!

I take a deep breath.

I get a good grip on the handle of my guitar case.

And I march out the door and down the stairs and straight into the kitchen.

"'Morning!" I say, walking in on Bob and Lois.

I say it big and bright, so no one will notice the coffin I'm carrying.

But it doesn't work.

They notice.

"'Morning," says Bob, looking up from his paper— looking at the coffin.

"Good morning," says Lois, looking up from her yogurt and raisins—looking at the coffin.

"Friday," I announce, trying to keep it big and bright.

But I can hear it ringing a little hollow in my ears.

Bob and Lois look up from the coffin.

They look at me.

They look at each other.

Bob goes back to his paper.

Lois goes back to her yogurt and raisins.

Happy to settle for a standoff, I stash my guitar in the corner and go to the counter and start fixing myself a bowl of cereal.

"Ah!" says Bob. "A good night for the Red Sox."

"Oh?" says Lois.

"Yeah," says Bob. "They got rained out. If you're a Red Sox fan, that's about as close as you get to winning."

"Really?" says Lois.

"Not really," Bob confesses.

"Oh," says Lois, smiling and giving him the laugh he was after.

Meanwhile, I've got my cereal together and I've joined them at the table.

Except—since I'm ahead of the game, at least so far—I've decided to be Invisible.

The way I've decided to be Invisible is by getting Totally Involved in my cereal.

And the milk—

And the spoon—

And my fingers, holding the spoon—

And my hand, lifting the spoon to my mouth—

And—

"You're going to your guitar lesson?"

It's Lois! Across the table. Talking to me. The jig is up.

"Yeah," I tell her.

I try to sound matter-of-fact, as if I couldn't care less.

"Elvis?" asks Bob.

His matter-of-fact puts my matter-of-fact to shame.

"I guess," I shrug.

Bob looks at Lois.

She's looking at me.

But now she looks down at her yogurt and raisins.

She scoops up a spoonful.

She puts it in her mouth.

She chews it up.

She swallows.

Then she looks at me again.

"Be careful," she says.

But she doesn't say it like a warning.

She says it like advice.

Like she's concerned.

"He'd better be careful!" says Bob.

And *he* says it like a warning.

Which is pretty surprising.

Even to Lois.

And I look over at Bob—blinking his eyes and ducking back behind his paper.

"*He's surprised, too!*" I think.

And I look over at Lois, who's gone back to fiddling with her yogurt and raisins.

"*People,*" I think, "*even the ones you know best— people are definitely weird!*"

Seventeen

"Pushed and pulled, hither and fro . . ."

"Different loyalties . . ."

"Toward Mum and Dad, and to your beau and to yourself, too . . ."

"Very loyal to yourself . . ."

"Your first loyalty . . ."

I'm climbing the stairs, on my way to The Eddie Nova Guitar Institute. On my way to my guitar lesson. On my way to Michael.

"But at least you'll never regret living by the lights of others. And you'll never regret not living at all.

"Lots of people do, you know. But—for good or ill—you're not one of them. . . .

"Do you see?"

"What do you think?" he says, greeting me as I open the door to Eddie Nova's reception area.

"Michael!"

He's sitting behind Eddie Nova's desk, looking like he owns the place.

56

"Where's Eddie?" I ask him.

"Giving a lesson," he says. "He left me in charge. So what do you think?"

Michael stretches back in Eddie's chair, puts his feet up on the desk and knocks the ash off an imaginary cigar.

"What you're looking at," he says—sounding like the guy who sells you the complete works of Elton John and a five-thousand-piece dinnerware set for $3.98 in between sections of "The Incredibly Late Show"—"is the chance of a lifetime! A chance to invest your money in a business with a real future. Think of it. A Guitar Institute of your very own! And—if you act now—there's still time to get in on the ground floor!"

"Second floor," I correct him.

"It is now," he says. "But the building's still settling."

The way he says it, there's nothing to do but laugh. Which I do.

And at the same time, I get myself ready to make my Fateful Decision.

Loving Michael the way I do, I know there's no other choice.

"What time are you picking me up tomorrow?" I ask him.

"Seven?" he asks.

"Sure," I tell him.

He smiles and starts getting up from Eddie's desk.

"Ready?" he says.

I tell myself, "I'd better be."

Except I say it out loud.

"Huh?" he says.

"Nothing," I tell him.

"Weird," he says, smiling at me and shaking his head.

"You don't know the half of it," I tell him.

Eighteen

Last night when I was lying in bed in the dark, waiting
for sleep to come, I played the guitar lesson over in my
head. . . .
Michael—
Walking with me down the hallway to our practice
room—
Opening the door for me—
A shy kind of grin on his face—
Closing the door—
Surprised to see me—
Just standing there—
Inside the door—
Waiting for him—
Praying for him—
To kiss me.
"Jess!"
"Oh, Michael!"
His hands, reaching out to me—
His eyes, shining down at me—

His mouth—
My mouth—
His tongue—
My tongue—
His mouth—
My mouth—
His eyes—
His hands—
Releasing me.
"Down to business. Work to do," he says.
"Right."
Guitars and music—
Love in his eyes—
Love in my eyes—
Laughing together—
Over my mistakes—
Over his jokes—
Music and guitars—
Laughter and love—
Guitars and music—
Love and laughter—
"Another lesson, coming up," he says.
"I have to run," I tell him.
"'Night, Jess."
"Thanks, Michael."
I stand, cross the room, pack up my guitar—
He sits at the window, strumming his guitar—
Something pretty—
Something new he's working on—
My guitar packed, I walk back to where he sits,
strumming—
"Like it?" he says. "It's gonna be a bear. . . . If I ever
get it worked out. . . . It's got something to do with
you."
I smile—
Bend down—
Kiss him—
Sweetly—

59

Gently—
"Good night, Michael."
"Want to try that again?"
I straighten and stand—
Just for a moment—
Swimming in his eyes—
Bathing in his smile—
Loving him—
I shake my head—
Turn—
Walk away—
Hoping he won't notice the way my head is bob-
bling around at the end of my neck—
Or how, when I reach the door, I have trouble turning
the damned doorknob! Anyway—

I played the guitar lesson over in my head, last night, when I was lying in bed, in the dark, waiting for sleep to come.

I played it over, and then I made my Final Decision.

"Sometimes," I reasoned, "telling the truth does a lot more harm than good. Not just to you. But to the very people you promised to tell the truth to. So if telling the truth—like that I'm going out with Michael tomorrow night, for example—if that upsets people and causes them more grief than a lie would, isn't it better and kinder, and isn't it right to lie?"

Last night, it seemed clear to me that it was.

It seemed clear that I'd save everybody—myself included—a lot of wear and tear if I just told Bob and Lois that I was spending Saturday night at Genevieve Roget's surprise pajama party.

I knew I could count on Genny—and on Caroline, who'd be there—to cover for me if Bob and Lois tried to check up on where I was.

Which they wouldn't do, anyway.

But if they did—if worse came to worst—somebody could always call me at The County Line. And I could drop everything. And I could get Michael or somebody to drive me over to Genny's, right away—before Bob and Lois showed up, demanding an in-person interview with their own precious daughter.

Otherwise—if everything worked out—when our date was over, I could just ask Michael to drop me off at Genny's.

I'd join the party—already in progress—spend the night clowning around, and go home the next day.

At home—no wiser but no sadder—Bob and Lois would welcome me with warm smiles and open arms, and our lives together would go rolling merrily along.

Last night, I made a note to call Michael in the morning so we could work out another place to meet.

Under the circumstances, I didn't think Michael's picking me up at home seemed like such a good idea.

And then—last night—satisfied that I'd finally made the right decision, I played the guitar lesson over in my head again.

Michael—

Walking with me down the hallway to our practice room— Opening the door for me— A shy kind of grin on his face—

Nineteen

Last night was the first thing I thought of when I woke up this morning.

Last night, I made my Final Decision.

And now, looking at the clear blue sky outside my window and the sunlight pouring into my room, I'm doubly sure I made the right decision.

So it's out of bed and into my sloppy jeans and my Dire Straits sweatshirt and down to the kitchen for a bracing cup of coffee.

Bracing is something I can use, right now—a little bracing to support the lie I'm about to tell.

Click-Click-Click.

Standing barefoot at the kitchen counter, sipping my coffee, I hear the sound of Grandma's hedge clippers.

Click-Click.

Moving to the window over the kitchen sink, I look out into the yard and see Grandma—dressed in her gardening clothes and her big old floppy sun hat with the narrow veil that ties beneath her chin—trimming the hedges.

Rap-rap-rap.

" 'Morning, Grandma!" I call, rapping at the kitchen window.

Grandma doesn't hear.

But it's okay.

To me, just seeing Grandma out there in the bright sunlight, hacking away at the hedges, is like the blue sky and the sunlight pouring into my room.

It's another good sign.

"Gemini," I think, "May 21 to June 21. Favorable conditions for lying."

I take another sip of coffee—for courage.

Then, turning away from the window and carrying my mug with me, like a lantern, I go off to spread the news—Jessie Walters, the Town Liar.

Lois is first.

Climbing the back stairs, I hear her music.

Lois always paints with music on—classical music, opera sometimes, whatever they're playing on either of the two stations that play that kind of thing.

The music sets a kind of peaceful mood for Lois and helps her get off into her painting place.

It sets a peaceful mood for me, too.

Even in the face of what I'm about to do.

Standing unnoticed in the doorway of the sunroom, I watch Lois—humming along with the music, dabbing her brush on her palette, rolling the bristles into a point, stroking the paint onto the canvas, delicately but firmly, just so.

I watch in silence.

Like a lion, stalking a grazing gazelle.

But watching her, I can't help thinking how really terrific Lois is.

And how lucky I am, having such a terrific person for a mother.

"What is it?" I ask her, very quietly, trying not to startle her.

"Oh!" says Lois, startled anyway.

"Sorry," I tell her.

"I guess I was way out there," Lois laughs.

And then, looking at her unfinished painting, she says, "I don't know. It's an abstract."

"It's pretty," I volunteer.

"You think so?" says Lois. "I was beginning to wonder."

"It looks like you," I tell her.

"You mean the morning after?" she laughs.

"No," I tell her. "The night before."

"Really?" she says, pleased to hear it.

But "the morning after" and "the night before" are both a little too close to the bone for me.

"Is Dad getting the papers?" I ask her, changing the subject.

"Mm," she says. "Why?"

She looks over at me, smiling and warm like she always is.

Except if I've hurt her.

Or disappointed her.

Or—

"We have to have a Summit Conference!" I tell her.

Don't ask me why.

I don't know why.

It just jumps out.

Bang!

There it is.

"Oh, no!" says Lois, looking like I've hurt her.

Or disappointed her.

Or—

Thrummm!

I hear the car in the driveway, below.

So does Lois.

Bob's home.

64

"All right," says Lois, angry already. "Let's get it over with!"

And she slaps her palette down on her table and tosses her paint brush into a glass.

"Excuse me," she says, brushing by me.

"Bob!" she calls.

And I just stand there, in the doorway, watching her walk away—

Knowing that sometimes the truth does more harm than good.

Knowing that this is definitely one of those times.

And knowing, nonetheless, that I'm about to tell Bob and Lois the truth—the whole truth—and nothing but the truth—so help me—

"Please, God, help me?"

"Jessie!"

It's Bob.

Calling me.

Angry already.

65

Twenty

Bob tosses the New York paper on the coffee table and drops into his chair.

"Okay, kiddo, what's it all about?"

"Well," says Jessie.

She looks over at Lois, leaning in the doorway, her arms folded across her chest.

"Mom?"

"I'm comfortable here," she says.

"Mom!"

"Lois," says Bob. "Come on. Be comfortable over here."

Lois sighs and says, "Okay."

And she walks to the chair at the other end of the coffee table.

And she plunks herself down.

And folds her arms across her chest.

Sitting alone at the center of the sofa, midway between Bob and Lois, Jessie doesn't look at either of them.

Instead, trying to concentrate, she studies her hands in her lap.

"I was going to lie to you," she says. "Again."

"About what?" Bob asks, evenly.

"The same damned thing," says Lois.

"Lois—"

"No," says Jessie. "She's right. It is the same thing."

"Oh," says Bob.

And he nods an apology to Lois.

"I thought we had that worked out," he says.

"We did," Lois insists.

"Only that I wouldn't lie about it again. Not that I wouldn't do it," Jessie tells Lois.

And then, turning to Bob, she finishes. "Go out with Michael, I mean."

"Oh, no!" says Lois, her voice rising. "We told you—"

"You told me," Jessie interrupts, her voice rising to top Lois's. "But I didn't agree!"

"Whoa!" shouts Bob, rising from his chair. "Hold on! This is talking we're doing here. Right? Instead of fistfights? Talking? Okay? . . . Okay?"

He looks at each of them, looking for their agreement. Then, satisfied that he has it—he drops back into his chair and, shaking his head, he says, "Worse than men, sometimes!"

"I'm sorry," says Jessie.

"Me, too," says Lois.

"You disagreed," says Bob, turning to Jessie. "When we said you were forbidden to see Michael, you disagreed with our decision."

Jessie nods her head and adds, "I still do."

"Do you know what 'forbidden' means?" Bob asks.

"It means you say I can't," Jessie answers.

"And if you do?" asks Lois.

"I guess you kick me out," says Jessie, dropping her eyes to her lap, "if you want to."

"We don't want to," Bob volunteers.

And he looks to Lois, inviting her to agree.

"You've made another date with Michael?" Lois asks.

"Tonight," says Jessie.

"Jessie!" says Bob, sounding surprised and hurt and angry.

"I didn't do it to spite you," Jessie explains. "I did it because . . . this is the first time I ever loved anybody. And . . . well . . . love's a very rare thing. Like, almost an endangered species. If it comes to you, you're not supposed to turn it away. You're supposed to take care of it. And protect it. Against everything. And everybody.

"Am I wrong?" she asks.

And she looks at them.

And she waits for an answer.

And Lois heaves a deep sigh.

"You've got the right idea," she admits.

And then, rising from her chair, she continues, "Anybody want anything from the kitchen? I'm going to make myself a Bloody Mary."

"I'll have a beer," says Bob.

"I want a Coke," says Jessie, rising from the sofa. "I'll help."

"No," says Lois. "That's all—"

"I'll help, too," says Bob, rising from his chair. "I don't want you two talking behind my back."

In the kitchen—observing an unofficial, unspoken and nonspeaking truce—they all fix their own drinks.

Then, following Lois's lead, they all take their regular chairs at the kitchen table.

"We're not against love here," says Bob, picking up the conversation. "In fact, we're in favor of it."

"I know," Jessie admits.

"It's just that there are some very real, very large problems with this particular instance of love," Bob continues.

"I know that too," Jessie confesses.

"And it's not just sex," says Lois. "Although that's more than enough, all by itself, to make you stop and think twice. But it's about your feelings too."

"What am I supposed to do about them?" Jessie asks helplessly.

Lois shakes her head and sighs.

"Be smart about them, I guess," she says. "Don't invest them in . . . well . . . fairy-tale princes, who—one day—just vanish in the air."

"Michael just looks like a fairy-tale prince," says Jessie. "He's a real person. And he really loves me. I don't think he'll vanish."

"Ever?" says Bob.

"I hope not," Jessie answers.

And Lois heaves another heavy sigh.

"If you see someone you love, riding for a fall," she says, "you're supposed to warn them."

"And if they won't listen?" Jessie asks.

"You pray for them," says Bob.

"And give them guidelines," Lois adds.

"You mean it's all right?"

"No!" shouts Bob. "It's not all right! Now that you ask. It stinks! And, to be honest, it makes me damned angry!"

And—just to prove his point—Bob slams his beer can down on the table.

He shoves his chair back and stands up and leans down over the table, staring Jessie right in the eye.

"It happens," he says, just barely keeping his temper under control, "it happens that I'm your father! And Lois, here, is your mother! And we not only know a hell of a lot more than you do—about everything—including love—but we're also responsible for you. Responsible *to* you. We're not going to let you turn yourself into some kind of minor-league groupie—who wakes up one day and finds herself sixteen years old and all used up. Wasted. Physically. And emotionally. I hear that kind of thing happens to a lot of very smart, very talented, very willful young girls these days."

"Michael's not—"

"I'm not finished!" he shouts. "Wait'll I'm through."

"But—"

"Jessie!" says Lois.

"We're *worried* about you," Bob shouts. "Do you understand *that?*"

"Yes," says Jessie.

"We think you've made a stupid mistake," he shouts, "and we're worried about you getting hurt."

"I appreciate it," says Jessie. "That you're worried. I'm worried, too."

"Good," says Lois.

His anger spent, Bob drops back down into his chair.

"Now," he says, "we can all worry together."

"I'm sorry," Jessie tells him.

"I want you home by midnight," he says.

"And if there's a problem," says Lois.

"Any kind of problem—" says Bob.

"We want to know about it," says Lois.

"Immediately," says Bob.

"I promise," says Jessie, feeling the tears welling in her eyes. "And . . . well . . . I just want you to know . . . you're the best—Excuse me!"

Racing against the sobs she feels heaving in her chest, Jessie stands and charges out of the kitchen.

Bob looks at the doorway.

He listens to his daughter racing up the front stairs, two steps at a time.

He looks across the table to Lois.

He sees she's crying.

He reaches across the table and takes her hand in his.

Lois looks at Bob.

She sees he's crying.

With her free hand, she reaches across the table and takes Bob's free hand.

They sit there, crying in silence, comforting each other with silence.

Twenty—one

It's hard to know how much makeup is enough. There's a real fine line between accenting what you've got and inventing what isn't there.

It's okay to cross the line if you don't mind looking like a punk rocker or a clown. But what I'm after at the moment is something else. I'm trying to look eighteen.

According to Michael, if you want to get into The County Line, you don't have to be eighteen. But you do have to look eighteen so you won't embarrass the guy from the State Liquor Authority when he comes around for his regular checkup and pay-off.

So that's why I'm putting on this opal-blue eye shadow, a thin layer at a time, building it up real gradually and trying to get as close as I can to looking eighteen without crossing the line.

If it wasn't for my face, I think I could get away with it.

In my boots and tight satin jeans, my Western blouse and my fringed suede vest, I think I could pass for an of-age young woman or even a well-preserved older woman.

It's my face that's the prob—

Gdongong!

The doorbell. Michael. I've got to go.

I promised Michael I wouldn't hang him up.

And it isn't fair to leave him alone with Bob and Lois for too long, either.

"Jessie!"

It's Bob, calling from downstairs.

"Yeah?" I shout.

"Michael wants to know how long!"

I don't answer right away.

Instead, very quickly, I turn away from my mirror and walk around in a tight little circle. When the circle takes me past the mirror, I catch a glimpse of myself out of the corner of my eye and—as if I were a stranger passing by—I ask myself, "What do you think of her makeup?"

"Not bad!" I think, catching a glimpse of myself-the-stranger in the mirror. "Hang on, Michael. Help is on the way."

As I hit the top of the stairs, I answer Michael's question. "How's now?" I say.

As I hit the landing, there he is—standing with Bob at the bottom of the stairs, looking up at me, smiling, loving me with his eyes—Michael!

And there—standing with Michael, looking quite a bit shorter and more uncomfortable than usual—stands Bob.

"Hi," says Michael.

"That was fast," says Bob.

Coming down the stairs to join them, I explain, "Michael's got a sound check."

"Oh, well," says Bob, "I suppose if you've got to have a check, a sound one is better than a rubber one."

Recognizing corn when he sees it, Michael laughs and shakes his head and says, "I guess."

"Don't you look terrific!" says Lois, looking down at me from the landing, halfway up the stairs.

"Thanks," I say.

"Evening," says Michael, greeting her with a smile.

Returning Michael's smile with an almost convincing smile of her own, Lois says, "Good evening," and she comes down the stairs to join us.

"Well," says Bob. "Not too late, now."

I've already promised Bob that I'll be home by midnight, but it's nice of him not to mention it.

"I'll bring her home right after the show," says Michael, nodding his head and giving Bob his assurance.

"Good," says Bob.

"Well," I say, leaning toward the door.

"Have a good time," says Lois.

"You, too," Michael tells her.

And he opens the door.

And I start for it.

But I stop before I get there.

I turn around and go back to Lois and hug her and say, "Thanks, Mom."

And then I hug Bob, and, hugging me back, he says, "I love you, too, kiddo."

And then he releases me.

And I turn and walk over to Michael and I take his hand.

Then, saying, "Good night," we walk out the door.

Together.

Me and Michael.

Michael and me.

Straight ahead.

Twenty–two

"Thar she blows!" says Michael, turning off the highway and bouncing into this huge empty parking lot that stretches back from the highway to The County Line.

The County Line is a long, low stucco building laced with planks of dark-stained wood, some of which form a frame for a big picture window with a sign advertising—

All Sports
Giant Screen
Cable TV

"They were Country-Western before," Michael explains as we bump across the asphalt. "But hardly anybody came. And I guess the ones who did show up spent the whole time drinking nothing but beer.

"So," says Michael, pulling around to the side of The County Line and heading toward a line of plastic

75

garbage cans that flank the club's back door, "while they're thinking about closing down for good, they figured they might as well try a little rock-and-roll. Except—since they haven't got any spare change to waste on advertising or anything—they haven't bothered telling anybody about it.

"So," he says, braking the wagon to a stop near the club's back door, "don't expect too much, okay?"

"They'll show up," I tell him.

"Well," he says, turning off the ignition and looking deep into my eyes, "at least you did."

I smile as he leans to kiss me.

"Hey!"

It's Mark, Michael's lead guitar, coming out The County Line's back door.

"Break it up!" he shouts at us.

"Did you see that?" he asks Leroy, who plays Michael's keyboards and who is, just now, coming out the door behind him. "Shocking!" he says.

"Okay, okay," says Michael, laughing and climbing out of the wagon. "Where's Arnie?"

"We've lost him, boss," says Mark, shaking his head.

"Sorry, Mike," says Arnie, suddenly appearing in the doorway with a grin on his face and his arm wrapped around the waist of a dark-haired waitress. "I got . . . uh . . . tied up. This is Angela. And she's taken. Right?"

Pulling Angela closer to him, Arnie gives her a big grin.

But Angela just laughs and spins away and—calling "Hi" to everybody—she turns and heads off into The County Line's dark interior.

Watching her as she struts away, Arnie shakes his head and turns to Michael and—wearing the face of a choirboy—he says, "Reminds me of my mother."

Everybody breaks up.

"Well," says Mark, turning to Michael, "you ready for the roadies?"

Michael smiles and nods his head.

And—like it's a signal—they all rear back and, at the top of their lungs, they shout "Roadies!"

Then everybody—Michael included—starts shouting, "Yes, boss!" and "Uh-huh!" and "Flying in!"

And Arnie starts singing, "Won't you sta-a-a-a-ay, just a little bit lon-ger-er . . ."

And everybody crouches down and scampers around to the back of Michael's wagon, where they throw the tailgate open and start hauling out all their equipment—what Michael calls their "amps and axes."

And I just stand there, watching and thinking, "If I was any happier, I'd probably explode."

Twenty–three

"Why don't I take you out front," says Michael, leading me through the kitchen at The County Line. "We'll find you a good spot before the crowd starts pouring in."

He says it with a smile on his face. He's not expecting anything like a crowd. But he's got things to do before the show and he'd rather not have me on his hands.

Which I understand.

So, taking Michael's hand, I follow him through the kitchen's swinging doors and into the club.

The club—

The County Line—

Six extremely long tables with an army of mismatched chairs pulled up to them—running almost the whole length of the room.

At one end of the tables is a little stage and a floor for dancing.

At the other end of the tables is a bar and, beyond that, The County Line's front door.

Michael leads me toward the stage end of the tables,

and as we pass the head of the table that's lined up with the center of the stage, he nods to it and smiles.

"Reserved for critics," he says.

I laugh and take the first chair, at the head of the next table—the spot Michael's picked out for me.

"I'll be looking for you," he says.

"Good luck," I tell him.

He bends and kisses me.

"I don't need luck," he says. "I've got you."

Sometimes, what Michael says and the way he looks at me makes me blush.

This is one of those times.

"Got to get to work," he says.

"Can't keep the crowd waiting," I tell him.

"Right," he smiles. And he turns and walks off toward the kitchen.

I sit for a while, watching the waitresses getting the place ready for the crowd, working out who works where, bustling around, setting up place settings in the spots they wind up with.

One of them winds up with me.

"Hi," she says, "I'm Giselle. You're with Michael?"

"Yes," I tell her.

She nods her head and smiles.

"Can I get you something?" she says.

Just dripping confidence, I tell her, "Uh . . . a beer?"

"You got I.D.?" she smiles.

The picture of maturity, I tell her, "Uh . . . I left it in my other pants."

She laughs.

"Where'd you leave *them?*" she says.

"Uh . . ."

She bends down, closer to me.

"Show me something," she says. "Anything."

And she gives me a wink.

I pry my wallet out of my satin jeans and show her my Student Government Card.

She takes it and looks at it. It says "John F. Kennedy Junior High School" across the top of it.

She hands it back to me.

"Heineken's all right?" she asks.

"Fine," I tell her.

"Comin' up," she says, and—giving me another wink—she turns and heads off toward the bar.

"Playing grown-up isn't all that easy," I tell myself. "But it's nothing I can't handle."

Then, I tell myself, "Sure, kiddo!"

And then, sitting there, all by myself, I break up laughing.

Twenty–four

"Evening, folks. I'm Paul Aaron Luscher. I'm what you might call your host. Or anything else you've got a mind to. Excepting only, late for supper . . ."

He's this neat round little man—wearing rimless glasses, a Western polyester suit and a string tie.

Everybody in the "crowd"—the men, at least—looks just like him. Neat and round and either middle-aged or trying to pass for it.

The women—dressed mostly in high-heeled boots, swingy short skirts, Western shirts and laminated hairdos—look a little younger and a little less real than the men.

"We got a special treat for y'all tonight. Something a little different from what you might be expecting . . ."

Altogether, the whole "crowd" doesn't quite fill a quarter of the room.

There are maybe fifty of us, and we're all sitting up close to the stage.

The rest of the room just stretches empty, all the way over to the bar.

"Larry? Could I get you to cut off the jukebox for me? . . . Thank you. What do these folks need with records, anyway, when we got the real live thing sitting right back here—"

"Jessie!"

"Me?" I wonder.

I look around and, coming toward me from the other end of the room, I see Karen—this hippy-dippy red-head I met once at one of Michael's rehearsals.

She looks real surprised to see me and, like she's congratulating me, she raises her fist in the air and calls, "Staying power!"

Then she turns and calls to somebody straggling along behind her, "Hey! Over here!"

The next thing I know, Karen's dropped into the chair across from me. She smiles and reaches across the table and squeezes my hand and says, "How y' doin'?"

"So if you're all ready now, The County Line is proud to present one of the best darned home-grown rock-and-roll bands in the whole darned rockin'-and-rollin' Meteropolitan Area! Englewood's own Skye Band!"

As everybody walks out onto the stage—everybody but Michael, who's supposed to come out later—

As they come out and pick up their instruments and start doing a little last-second tuning up—

I clap and shout.

And so does Karen.

And so do her three friends, who've squeezed in at the table with us.

But we're the only ones!

The rest of the crowd just sits there and watches!

I look across the table to Karen.

She glances around the room, gives a little shiver

and—real quiet, like she doesn't want anyone else to hear—she whispers, "Creepy!"

On the stage, the tuning up is over.

His back to the crowd, Mark counts, "One—two—one, two, three *and*—!"

Gung-Gung-Gung-Gung!

Like a freight train heating up, getting ready for the race up the mountain and the liftoff into the sky, The Skye Band comes out smoking and spitting fire!

We whoop and shout!

Me and Karen and her three friends.

And everybody else?

They just sit there!

Flinching at the sound pouring out of the speakers.

Wondering what on earth's gone wrong around here.

Gung-Gung-Gung!

But The Skye Band keeps cranking it up!

Gung-Gung!

I look over at the bar, where all the waitresses are gathered in a bunch.

Looking at the stage and watching the crowd, they're all giggling and laughing among themselves.

But there's no stopping it now!

Gung!

Michael's there!

There with the song!

Wailing it!

Shouting it!

At the center of the stage!

Now, some folks like it nice and warm.
But me—I like it hot.
So, if you're with me, stick around,
And we'll get down to Rock Bottom.

Rock Bottom's nowhere on the map.
Can't get it on the phone.

Rock Bottom dance halls rock all night.
Rock Bottom is my home. . . ."

And on and on.
Better and better.
Sometimes so sweet.
Sometimes so hot.
Wonderful!
Gung-Gung-Gung-Gung!
With a lift of his knee and a slash of his hand across
his guitar, Michael sets off the song's final chord—a
mile-high wall of sound that climbs straight up, then
cuts off abruptly and flutters down to the ground.

"Wow!" I shout, jumping to my feet and clapping my
brains out!
Karen claps, too.
But sitting down.
And her friends clap.
And a couple of others.
Two or three.
Nobody else.
"Nuts!"
Somebody says it real loud and real disgusted.
And he gets a big laugh.
"Creepy," Karen whispers.
"Maybe you folks are looking for something a little
softer and sweeter," says Michael, smiling and trying to
win the crowd over. "More like soft ice cream. Instead
of fire and ice. Am I right?"
"Nuts!"
Michael smiles at the guy and he nods his head at him
and he says, "This is for you."
I look at Karen.
She shrugs.
Michael turns to the band and says, "Maybellene."
Karen giggles.
Michael counts, *"One,* two, three *and—"*
BRrrraaannNG!

Chuck Berry's "Maybellene" comes whip-sawing out of Michael's guitar—

Strutting, proud and uppity, all around the room. Like she owns the place. And what's all this white trash doing around here, anyway? Running down her fine neighborhood!

"Nuts!"

Him again!

"Expected to hear music!"

Somebody else.

Now they're standing up.

More than a few of them.

And the women with them.

They're not waiting for their checks or anything.

They're just walking out.

While Michael and the band are up there, singing and playing and trying not to notice.

But they're walking out.

It's awful!

And it stays awful.

Through six more songs.

And then, because what's left of the crowd responded to the band's last song with dead silence, Michael announces an *encore!*

What's left of the crowd takes the news with an assortment of coughs, chair scrapes and muttered conversations.

Michael gathers the band together at the back of the stage and, on his cue, they break into "Red River Valley"— *From this valley they say you are going . . .* That one!

And—even though they've probably never played the song together before—the band plays it straight through, making up a really pretty arrangement as they go along.

And Michael sings it all the way through, too, singing it soft and pretty and making the song's sad story true.

85

And when the song is over, what's left of the crowd applauds.

Just when I was thinking they didn't know how to!

And Michael grins his grin and says, "Thank you very much, ladies and gentlemen. Be sure to stick around for the second show."

And then the crowd claps a little more as Michael and the band leave the stage.

I turn to Karen and say, *"Second* show?"

"Yeah," she says, "we've got about an hour to kill. Want to go out back and get high?"

I don't want to know the answer, but I've got to ask.

"What time is it?"

"About eleven," she says.

I push my chair back from the table.

"Where you going?" she asks.

As I get up from the table, I tell her, "I have to turn myself in to the man from the State Liquor Authority. I need to be put in protective custody."

"Say what?"

I put three dollars down on the table to cover the cost of my beer. As I do, I tell Karen, "It's a terrible problem. A personal tragedy."

"Oh," she says, offering me her sympathy.

"Yeah," I tell her. "Thanks."

"If there's anything I can do," she says.

"If only you could," I think and—declining her offer with a wave—I turn and take off, heading for the swinging doors, the kitchen, Michael's dressing room and—one way or another—home.

Twenty-five

The dressing room door is closed.

I knock.

Behind the door, somebody shouts, "Yeah?"

Somebody else shouts, "Nobody's home!"

Then the door opens a crack, and Emily peeks out at me.

"Oh," she says, opening the door and introducing me. "Another mourner."

It gets a laugh.

Inside the dressing room, everybody's not as depressed as you'd think they'd be.

It's more like they're angry, and looking for a way to laugh it off.

Michael—glistening with sweat, a towel draped around his neck—Michael gives me this kind of sorry-but-I-warned-you smile and walks over to me and takes my hand and, real quiet, he says, "In Atlanta, one time, we were playing in this German beer hall, and they started tossing beer steins at us. We ducked the first few. But after that, we started picking them up and throwing them back. It's just rock-and-roll, Jess. It comes with the territory. Right, guys?"

"Right!" says Mark, jumping to attention and throwing Michael a snappy salute.

"Right!"

"Right!"

"You bet!"

Except for Arnie, everybody jumps to attention.

"Now," says Michael, pacing around the tiny room like a drill sergeant addressing his troops. "Who's got *The Roy Rogers Songbook?*"

"'Red River Valley'?" says Arnie, shaking his head like he can't believe it.

"Pretty tune," says Mark, defending it.

"Yeah but—come on!" says Arnie. "We're supposed to be a rock-and-roll band!"

"Yeah," says Mark. "But who says, 'Red Riv—'?"

"Hey!" says Michael, cutting off the discussion. "That was just a strategic retreat. What they call advancing to the rear. I was just trying to buy us a little time so we could get back here and regroup."

"When we go back out there again," he says, "I want to make sure everybody's ready."

"Ready to what?" says Arnie.

Michael smiles and throws his head back and screams, "Rock and roll!"

And everybody else joins in, screaming, "Rock and roll!" and "All right!" and "Eeeeeeeehaw!"

And Michael turns to me—looking as happy as I've ever seen him—and he puts his hands around my waist and lifts me up in the air and spins me around and brings me down to a long, happy kiss.

"Rock and roll!"

"All night long!"

"Whoooeee!"

Back on the floor, I open my eyes and say, "Michael? Can we—?"

And I nod my head toward the door.

"The kitchen?" says Michael.

He looks perplexed.

"Yeah," I tell him. "Or—"

He doesn't get it.

"What's up?" he says.

I step a little closer to him and drop my voice to a whisper.

"It's a kind of disease," I tell him. "Hereditary. If I don't get enough sleep, I fade. To dust. I just—"

"Funny," he says.

But he doesn't think it's funny.

"I promised, Michael. They made me."

"Promised?" he says, shaking his head.

He's getting impatient with me.

"I have to be home by twelve," I whisper.

"Twelve?" he shouts.

He doesn't shout it. He says it—real loud. And angry.

Everybody stops talking.

Everybody looks.

Somebody snickers.

Michael just stares at me.

I just stare back at him.

"We're on again in about forty-five minutes," he says, talking to me one word at a time, like he's explaining something to a child. "Englewood's a half hour each way!"

"I'll call a taxi," I tell him.

He just glares at me.

"I'll take her," says Arnie, hoping it's a joke.

It isn't.

Not to Michael.

"I'll take her," he says.

"Hey," says Mark, angry and objecting.

But Michael's got my wrist.

And he's already dragging me out the door.

And through the kitchen.

And out the back door.

And into the parking lot.

And into his car.

Slam!

Slam!

Peeling out.

Nobody saying a word.

On the highway.

Heading home.

Fast.

Radio blasting away.

Tears in my eyes.

No!

Fighting them back.

He promised!

"You promised!" I remind him, trying to keep my voice under control, trying to keep the tears out of it. "You promised you'd . . . share . . . share the hassle . . . of me . . . being young . . . and us . . . going . . . slow."

He looks over at me.

Looks into my eyes.

"Well," he says.

And I see the smile beginning to bloom across his face, as he returns his eyes to the road, and—

"Damn!" he says.

A flashing light.

Behind us.

A police car.

After us.

Still smiling, Michael pulls the wagon over to the side of the road.

"I hope you're willing to share the hassle of goin' fast!" he says.

Which breaks me up.

And him, too.

"Registration," says the policeman.

And the curtain falls on—

Our First Fight . . .

Twenty–six

"If I don't get another ticket on the way back," says Michael, "I should clear twenty or thirty bucks on the night."

He says it like a joke.

And he smiles when I laugh.

We're parked in front of my house, and Michael's pocket watch—resting on the dashboard in front of us—says it's twenty-five minutes to twelve.

"I wonder," says Michael. "If Bob Seger knew the kind of money we're pulling down at The County Line, do you suppose he'd be wasting his time playing at Madison Square Garden?"

"Maybe he figures he owes it to his fans," I suggest.

"Yeah," Michael smiles. "That could be it."

And he laughs.

And he puts his arm around me and draws me close to him.

I start to tell him how sorry I am for messing up a perfectly rotten night.

"I wish—"

"Shhh . . ." he whispers.

And he kisses me, kisses me, kisses me—

Pressing hard against me—

His hands—

His fingers—

Caressing my back—

Pressing me hard against him—

Kissing me, kissing me, kissing me—

Forever—

And ever—

'Til Death do us—

"Oh, Michael!"

I gasp for breath and snuggle my head against his chest.

Closing my eyes—so happy—I feel his chest expanding as he takes a deep, deep breath.

Now—letting it out in a long, long sigh—he says, "Gotta go."

"Mmm," I tell him.

But I don't budge.

He laughs.

"Jess?"

"Okay, okay."

I sit up.

"Talk to you tomorrow," he says.

"If you make it through the second show," I remind him.

He looks at his pocket watch.

"If I make it *to* the second show," he says.

I lean over and give him a quick kiss good night.

"Good night," I say, reaching for the door.

"Jess?"

"Huh?"

Giving me his warmest, sexiest smile, he says, "Someday I'd like to hear you say 'good morning.'"

For a second, I forget how to breathe.

But then it comes back to me.

"Sure," I say.

And I lean back and kiss him again—real quick.

Then I smile and say, "Good morning!"

As I open the door and climb out of the car, Michael laughs and calls, "Thanks."

Then—without waiting to hear "You're welcome"— he shifts into gear, pops the clutch and goes zooming off down the street.

I watch him until he's out of sight.

Then, I turn and walk to the house.

I climb the stairs and let myself inside.

No one's waiting up for me.

They're all upstairs.

Sleeping.

"Nice," I think.

Turning off the downstairs lights, I tiptoe up the stairs.

As I reach the top of the stairs—

"Good night"—

Bob calls softly from behind his bedroom door.

Startled, I catch my breath and answer, " 'Night."

"Good night," Lois calls softly.

" 'Night."

"Good night already!" Grandma bellows, loud and clear.

I laugh and bellow back, "Good night, Grandma!"

And then I'm into my room.

And into my bed.

And—closing my eyes—I'm back in Michael's arms.

Twenty–seven

In a way, it's the guitar lessons that keep me half sane.

That's how it is these days—I'm half sane and half crazy.

No.

Worse than that.

When I'm sane, I'm completely sane.

When I'm crazy, I'm completely crazy.

So it's more like I'm two people.

Me and the other me.

Me and *The Other Jessie.*

But me first.

A lot of the time, I'm just me—like I've always been.

I'm me at school and I'm me at home and I'm me going back and forth between different places.

But where I'm me most is Mondays and Fridays, after school.

At my guitar lessons.

Usually, what happens is, as I walk into our practice

95

room, Michael's sitting over by the window, playing his guitar.

Mostly, he's playing what he calls my "theme."

It's the song he said he was working on—the one he said had something to do with me—the one that's going to be a bear if he ever gets it worked out.

That one.

Real pretty.

A little sad.

And strange.

I never interrupt him.

Interrupt my own theme?

No.

I just close the door as quietly as I can.

I unpack my guitar from its case as quietly as I can.

And then, as quietly as I can, I walk across the room to where Michael's sitting, near the window.

He looks up from his guitar, smiles and says, "Hi."

I say, "Hi."

And I lean down and kiss him.

Sweetly.

Tenderly.

Not long.

But lingering.

Just long enough.

Just deep enough.

And then the lesson begins.

And it's just plain terrific.

Because we're better with each other.

Easier and more relaxed than we were before.

And because I'm getting better at playing my guitar.

I'm not good.

But I'm getting better.

Especially at the first stuff Michael taught me—the easiest stuff.

When I strum the basic chords now, it doesn't sound like I'm actually playing—

But it doesn't sound like I'm just practicing, either.

The newer stuff Michael's taught me—the more difficult chords and chord progressions—I'm still real clunky and twangy at.

Like right now—

Michael's showing me how to play the *d minor* chord.

We've been playing through some of the easiest stuff together, but now we've stopped so he can show me the *d minor* chord.

"Like this," he says.

On the fretboard, his fingers look like a very confused pretzel.

And he's waiting for me to scrunch up my fingers into the same very confused pretzel on my fretboard.

Ha!

"Too hard?" he says, giving himself away with a smile.

He knows it's too hard.

That's the point!

"It's a real handy chord," he says. "No home should be without one."

He wants me to learn it.

Okay. I'll learn it.

I do my scrunch-fingered version of the very confused pretzel on my fretboard and then, closing my eyes, I turn away and strum.

What can I say?

The inventor of the *d minor* chord will never forgive me.

I've turned his beautiful *d minor* into a *Major Discomfort*.

Forgive me, Sir or Madam—I know not what I do.

I open my eyes to see Michael looking at me and fighting very hard not to laugh out loud.

Among guitar teachers, this is considered very unprofessional.

Good!

I start strumming my *Major Discomfort* chord in rhythm and, looking over at Michael, I say, "Wanna dance?"

That does it!

Michael bursts out laughing with a yelp that springs him up from his chair and sends him reeling around the room, laughing like a maniac.

Serves him right!

Michael's reeling brings him around to where I'm sitting, and collapses him to his knees on the floor at my feet.

Raising his arms, he drapes his hands over my shoulders, looks up at me and—still laughing—he says, "Time's up."

Which makes me laugh.

But the second I stop, I see Michael—no longer laughing, just looking up at me, looking up into my eyes.

That's when it happens!

Right then!

When we're kissing goodbye—

Deeper than hello.

Deep enough to last us.

Deep enough to last us while we're apart.

That's when the half-sane part of me shouts—

"No!"

"It's too soon!"

"You're not ready!"

That's when the half-sane part of me realizes—

She's not listening!

Won't listen!

Can't listen!

That's when the half-sane part of me panics and flees.

That's when—

At that exact moment—

The Other Jessie—

Her bag in her hand—

Looks up—
Sees the "Vacancy" sign—
And moves right in.
The Other Jessie can't get enough of Michael.
She wants his mouth, tongue, her fingers in his hair,
her back arching—!
All of him!
Now!
Everything!
Now!
Michael! . . . Michael! . . .
"Michael! . . . Michael?"

"Huh?"

"You've got a lesson," I remind him.

Me. The sane one. Jessie. I've moved back into my
room at the Jessie Walters Motel.

The Other Jessie has checked out. She's left no
forwarding address. But they're expecting her back any
time now.

"Michael? . . . Lesson?"

"Mm," he nods.

He's still kneeling on the floor in front of me. But
now—leaning back, his arms dangling at his sides, his
head thrown back, his eyes closed—he's fighting to
catch his breath, to control his breathing.

"What?" he gasps, eyes still closed. "What time?
Tonight? Seven?"

"Yeah," I tell him.

Me.

Jessie.

"Should be fun," I tell him.

And I stand up—me—and I cart myself and my
guitar over to the piano bench near the door, where
I've left my guitar case.

When my guitar's packed up and I'm ready to go, I
ask Michael, "You okay?"

He's still the way I left him.

Except now, he's smiling and breathing normally.

But his eyes are still closed.
Nodding his head, he says, "Mm."
I say, "Okay. See you tonight, then."
"Mm."
And I walk out the door.
Not knowing when *The Other Jessie* will show up again.
But knowing she will.
Like it or not.
Sooner or later.

Twenty-eight

The reason why I'm going out with Michael tonight—
Friday—instead of tomorrow night is—

Tomorrow night, Michael and The Skye Band are
playing a high-school dance in Oradell.

The dance is called "Summer Thunder."

It's supposed to celebrate the approach of summer
and summer vacation.

But everybody's supposed to come dressed in rain-
wear.

Also, the dance doesn't break up until 2:00 A.M.,
which—according to Michael—usually means about
two-thirty or even three.

Well—

Since I'm not crazy about boogying in my raincoat
and galoshes with a bunch of high-school kids I've
never met—

And since I've already decided to put off asking Bob
and Lois the extremely tricky "Next time, can I stay for

the second show?" question—at least until there's an actual second show to stay for—

I suggested to Michael that we go out tonight.

And when Michael told me he was planning to meet the band tonight—to set up their amps and axes and microphones in the gym at the high school where they're playing tomorrow—

I told him, "Sounds like fun."

I told myself, "At least I won't have to wear my galoshes."

And the way it turns out, it is fun.

Up to a point.

What's fun is—

Hanging out in this big dark empty gymnasium.

Having the whole dark haunted school to ourselves.

Me and Michael and Mark and Arnie and Lenny and Leroy and Emily.

And this guy from the Dance Committee.

And this caretaker, who's supposed to know where all the outlets and switches and things are.

Except he doesn't.

So—

We have to figure it out for ourselves.

Which we do.

We get the lights on in the gym.

We get all the equipment—the amps and axes and microphones—set up and tested.

And then—

When everything's checked out and ready to roll—

But it's still only about ten-thirty—

Everybody gets hit with this sudden inspiration to start rehearsing, right away, here and now.

Everybody—that is—but Michael.

Which isn't like him.

And everybody—including me—knows it.

Michael does his best to convince everybody he's got good reasons for resisting their sudden inspiration.

102

If they put off rehearsing until tomorrow, like they planned, the band can use tomorrow's rehearsal as a warm-up for the dance.

And rehearsing tonight and then warming up tomorrow, before the dance, is like too much of a good thing.

Those are Michael's reasons.

The ones he says.

But everybody—including me—knows they aren't his real reasons.

His real reason is me.

His wanting to be with me.

Tonight.

Now.

And, without anybody saying anything, everybody—including me—agrees that's reason enough.

Out in the parking lot—after a lot of last-minute joking and clowning around—the party breaks up.

Everybody piles into two cars, and they start up and they drive off.

Michael and I are left standing alone in the dark silence of the night, under a sky full of stars.

Smiling at me—almost shyly—Michael takes my hand and leads me around to my side of the wagon.

Opening the door for me—like a chauffeur—he says, "Miss Walters," and he bows.

As I move past him, Michael reaches out and takes my arm and—drawing me to him—he kisses me.

Her bag in her hand—
The Other Jessie Walters looks up—
Sees the "Vacancy" sign—
And moves right in.
Sitting with Michael.
On the service road.
Up behind the high school.
Looking down on the parking lot.
Looking out over the lights of the town.
The Other Jessie turns and—

"Jess!"—

From behind the wheel of the wagon, Michael smiles over at her.

Reaches out to her.

Draws her to him.

Slides her under him.

Her body.

A thousand wishes come to life.

A thousand wishes hungering to be fulfilled.

Now!

All of him!

Now!

Everything!

One.

Long.

Continuous.

First him.

Then her.

Now this way.

Now that.

Bodies.

Pressing.

Pressing together.

Now her.

Now him.

That way.

This.

Tongues.

Plunging.

Hips.

Thrusting.

"Oh!"

"Jess!"

"Oh!"

"Jessie!"

His hand!

Inside her blouse.

His fingers.

104

Caressing my—!

"Michael! No! Please!

"Michael! Stop!"

"Jess!"

"Please!"

"Damn!"

Slowly.

His eyes shut tight.

Michael lifts himself up.

Quickly.

He turns, opens his door, jumps out of the wagon.

Sitting up, I see him through the open door, walking off a few paces, stopping, stretching, shouting— "Whoa!"—up at the sky.

I see his hand, reaching around behind him, tucking his shirt into the back of his pants—moving around in front of him, arranging—

I look away.

I have myself to arrange.

I have to pull myself together.

Button my blouse.

Tuck it in.

Comb my hair.

Fix my makeup.

"Sorry," he says.

I'm arranging my hair in his rearview mirror.

He's leaning down, looking in the open window at me, smiling.

I try to explain.

"Michael, I—"

"I know," he says, shushing me gently, with a lift of his hand. "Take you home?"

"Please," I tell him.

He nods his head and—turning his back to me—he looks up at the sky once more.

He sighs deeply and says, "Pretty night."

"Yeah," I tell him. "Very."

Twenty–nine

The Truth About Teen-age Sex!

There is none.

I don't mean sex.

I mean truth about it.

Or else, there are so many truths about teen-age sex, there might as well be none.

Some teen-agers do.

Some teen-agers don't.

That much, I'm pretty sure of.

Are those who do better off than those who don't?

Are those who don't better off than those who do?

What do you think The President of the United States is doing, right this second?

Who knows?

Not me.

All I know is, it's real hard making your way through heavy traffic when you don't know whether you're traveling fast or slow.

I think I'm slow.
For my age.
I'm not bragging.
Believe me.
Fast is in fashion.
Hardly anybody pretends they're slow anymore.
At least, in public.
But even if I don't count all the teen-aged girls who wound up at spring training camp with the Pittsburgh Steelers, or the ones who bumped into Mick Jagger on the plane to Akron or Bruce Springsteen on the bus going into Newark—even if I don't count them, I still think I'm probably slow.
Even when I was pretending to Michael that I was sixteen—
Even when I looked more or less like I might be sixteen—
I couldn't act sixteen.
I couldn't act fourteen.
I think I'm slow.
Not that I'd admit it to anybody but myself.
But if you can't admit a thing like that to yourself, who can you admit it to?
I admit it.
I'm slow.
It's embarrassing to admit.
But I admit it.
I mean, there's this Sexual Revolution going on, and here I am a Conscientious Objector!
No.
That's not true.
It's not a matter of conscience, my being slow.
It's not like I think there's something wrong with sex. Or sex before marriage. Or sex before a certain age.
I don't.
Honestly.
I think sex is right and good and beautiful.
I could do a commercial for it.

Except I'm not all that familiar with the product.

Which doesn't mean I'm completely unfamiliar with it.

It's not like I've never read a book or seen a movie or played Spin the Bottle, or anything.

And a couple of times I've had, like, *crushes* on different boys.

And once (or twice, maybe) I did let one (or maybe two) of these boys I had crushes on kiss me and hold me and stuff.

And even though it felt mostly awkward and embarrassing, it didn't always feel *so* awkward and embarrassing that I couldn't also feel the pleasure of being kissed and held and stuff.

I could.

And I did.

And I do.

And I'm grateful.

Because I know not everybody has felt the pleasure of those things.

But with Michael—

It's beyond feeling the pleasure.

It's into wanting to feel the pleasure.

Even needing to.

And when my Needing and Michael's Needing lock into each other, Needing takes us over and sends us spinning off into a Universe where Nothing is enough.

And Everything is inevitable.

Everything!

That's what I'm really scared of.

That's what I can't imagine.

I mean, Michael's very large.

All over.

And I'm not that large.

Any place.

And—

It scares me, that's all!

And I'm real sorry it scares me.

In fact, I think it's a cheat.

I mean, let's face it, if you're like Michael—if you're that gorgeous and that sweet and smart and sexy—and if you can really rock-and-roll—there are an awful lot of girls out there who'd do Anything just to show you how much they're not afraid of sex.

Which probably means there are an awful lot of girls out there who have done Everything just to show Michael how much they're not afraid of sex.

Which definitely means, when Michael's with me, he knows what he's missing.

And he misses what he's missing.

And if I don't give him what he's missing—as much as he loves me—and I really believe he does—there are an awful lot of girls out there, etc.

What it comes down to is this—

Aside from being slow, I'd be pretty stupid if I lost Michael over something as right and good and beautiful as sex!

I mean, just because it's a little scary, is that any reason to—

I mean, it's not like there's anything especially wonderful about—

I mean, some of my best friends—

Or, at least, a few girls I know—

And almost all the grown-ups I know—

I mean, they don't seem like they've been totally destroyed by sex.

Quite a few of them seem like they're doing pretty well.

So what's the big deal?

Or am I just a chicken?

Bawk! Bawk! Bawk!

In the Interest of Science—and to find out where I really stand in the fast-slow order of things—I decide to conduct a Scientific Survey.

I decide to gather a Random Sampling of Teen-age Sexual Awareness, Attitudes and Practices.

By sheer coincidence—I assure you—the first person I interview on the subject turns out to be Caroline.

Imagine my surprise!

Anyway—

One day after school, I go home with Caroline.

The idea is—Caroline and I are going to hang out and do our homework together.

But so far, we haven't gotten to our homework.

We have gotten to Caroline's refrigerator, though.

And to Caroline's finished basement, where we are bopping around to the stereo and pigging it up.

Now—I know Caroline is pretty inexperienced, to say the most.

And I know she's a little uncomfortable talking about s-e-x.

But I've got my Scientific Survey to think about!

And so, sneaking into it, I say, "Caroline, do you ever imagine yourself? You know, like seeing a movie of yourself? In your head? Doing things? With a boy?"

"Like what?" she says. "Like riding horses?"

I might have known. This is going to get me no-where.

"Yeah," I say.

Not very enthusiastically.

"Yeah!" she says.

And she's all excited.

I remind myself, "You asked for it," and—plunging ahead—I say, "Really?"

"Yeah," she says, drifting off to Dreamland. "Me . . . and this . . . this guy . . . We're riding these horses . . . Arabians . . . One white . . . That's mine . . . And one black . . . That's his . . . We're riding along . . . Bareback . . .

"The horses?"

"Yeah," she says, missing my joke. And—taking me for a space cadet—she explains, "Without saddles."

Nodding my head as if I'd just been Celestially Enlightened, I say, "Uh-huh."

"We're riding down this beach," she says, "with all these huge, funny-looking rocks . . . with all these huge ocean waves pounding up against them . . ."

I wait for her to go on.

She doesn't.

"Is that it?" I ask her.

There's more. I can see it.

But Caroline's reluctant to go on.

"Well . . ." she says. "No . . . But . . ."

"What happens?" I ask her.

And now I'm all excited.

She shrugs her shoulders like it's no big deal.

"He takes me home," she says.

"And?"

"He kisses me good night."

"At the front door?"

"Of course!" she says, like "Anybody'd know *that!*"

"Is your mouth closed or open?" I ask her.

"Jessie!" she says, like she's shocked.

"Okay," I say, "is *his* mouth closed or open?"

"Jessie!"

This time it's more like she's warning me.

"It's only a movie." I tell her. "It's not even a real movie."

"I don't care!" she snaps.

"But Car—"

"It's none of your business!" she hisses.

She's wrong, of course.

It is my business.

It's the start of my Scientific Survey on Teen-age Sexual Awareness, Attitudes and Practices.

But, on the other hand, if Caroline doesn't want to invite me to see the thrilling climax of her movie, I really don't have a right to complain.

Especially since she's just caught me trying to sneak in.

So I tell her I'm sorry.

And I didn't mean to pry.

111

But I just happen to be interested in horses, lately.

Caroline invites me to come horseback riding with her.

I accept.

The first—and last—interview in my Scientific Survey comes to an end.

I realize now there's no point in going on with it.

I know the Truth About Teen-age Sex.

I am not as slow as some girls.

And I am not as fast as others.

And it's the others I've got to worry about.

Them and me.

Thirty

Sunday-morning music.

When I think about it, I usually think about church music—organs and choirs and things.

Or else, maybe, classical music—symphonies and operas.

Usually, I don't put Sunday morning together with rock-and-roll.

But here it is, a little after ten o'clock Sunday morning, and here I am, sitting downstairs in Mark's semifinished basement, and here's Michael and The Skye Band tuning up and—yes, Sunday-morning-music fans—it's time to rock-and-roll!

Or it will be, as soon as the McCarren brothers—P.J. and J.P.—as soon as they get themselves settled.

It's because of them that Sunday morning and rock-and-roll got put together in the first place.

The way Michael explained it to me in the wagon on the way over to Mark's, the McCarren brothers are a lot heavier than Paul Aaron Luscher or the guy from the Dance Committee in Oradell.

These people are actually in the rock-and-roll business.

The McCarren brothers—P.J. and J.P.—are the real McCoy.

They own a club in Elizabeth that presents two or three different rock-and-roll bands every night of the week.

The club is called Mr. E's, and I hear their ads on the radio all the time, along with the ads for all the other rock clubs.

The thing is, if The Skye Band got booked into Mr. E's and they did okay there, it probably wouldn't be too hard to go on to the other clubs that advertise on the radio—at least the smaller local ones.

Michael could wind up working all summer, getting professional experience and getting paid enough to put something away for school in the fall.

Michael's going to the University of Michigan, in Ann Arbor. To study music at their music school.

He told me a while ago.

But I try to forget it as much as I can.

He doesn't know how long he'll stay there. As long as it's interesting, he says.

He says there's too much he doesn't know about music, and the time to find out how much he doesn't know is now, while he's young and willing to take the time.

Anyway, he expects he'll be getting home for vacations, which colleges have a lot of, and long ones.

And maybe I could come out to see him in Ann Arbor, sometimes—for dances and things.

And a lot of other maybes.

Except for us.

Me and Michael.

We're for sure.

From now on, Michael says.

And I believe him.

As hard as I can.

Whenever I can't remember to forget about it.

About Michael's going off to Ann Arbor in September.

But Michael can't forget about it.

Because, for one thing, he has to pay for it.

At least, for part of it.

Which is why he's auditioning for the McCarren brothers—P.J. and J.P.—in Mark's basement this morning.

P.J. and J.P. McCarren are so busy running Mr. E's every night of the week, that Sunday morning is about the only time they have to listen to new bands.

So here they are, sitting in Mark's basement—which is The Skye Band's hard-times rehearsal studio—checking out the rumor (started by The Skye Band) that The Skye Band might be "ready."

But the McCarren brothers haven't got all day.

Three songs is all they've got time to listen to.

Michael picks a fast one to start, a real hard-rocking thing called "Dangerous Dudes."

Everybody gets into it good, so good it almost raises Mark's house off its foundation.

And when it's over, P. J. (or J. P.) says, "Okay," and nods his head up and down.

And J. P. (or P. J.) nods his head up and down and says, "All right."

Then Michael and The Skye Band do a slow one—"Shades of Blue"—which is so sad and pretty, it almost breaks your heart, the way Michael sings it.

In fact, it looks like it's more than the McCarren brothers can take, because—before the song's half over—they've stood up on their feet, waving for the band to stop playing.

"You free next Saturday?" P. J. (or J. P.) says.

"Yeah," says Michael.

115

"Okay," says J. P. (or P. J.). "Call me Monday. About six or seven. I'll tell you what time and how much."

"Hey," says Michael. "Thanks."

"How do we get back to the highway from here?" says P. J. (or J. P.).

"Who do I ask for when I call?" says Michael.

"P. J." says P. J. (or J. P.).

"Or J. P." says J. P. (or P. J.).

"I'll point you," says Mark, and—handing his guitar to Lenny—he leads the McCarren brothers up the stairs and out of the house to their waiting VW (or WV) (or whatever).

"Who cares?"

"Whooooooeeeeeeeeeee!"

"Rock and roll!"

It's eleven o'clock Sunday morning, and—yes, Sunday-morning-music fans—it's time to party!

Thirty-one

"Close the door," he says.

"Huh?"

"The door," he says. "Close it."

"Uh . . ."

The house is empty.

Mark's mother is a registered nurse, and she's out working today.

Mark's father has been living in Texas for the last couple of years.

And—when the beer ran out—Mark and the others decided to move the party to Arnie's for fresh supplies.

"We'll catch up with you later," Michael told Mark as everybody was heading out the door.

Mark smiled and told Michael, "Don't do anything I wouldn't do!"

Then he looked over at me—as if he hadn't noticed me standing there, right next to Michael—and he said, "Oops!" and he jumped up in the air and he ran out the door like he was being chased. Except he was laughing and waving back at us the whole time.

And Michael laughed.

And I laughed, too.

But I'm not laughing now.

"Jess . . ."

Michael's stretched out on the couch, across the room in this kind of den that's off in one corner of Mark's semifinished basement.

"Huh?"

He smiles and shakes his head.

"What are you thinking about?" he says.

"Your mother," I tell him.

He looks at me like I'm crazy.

And maybe I am.

But I figure, if I can get Michael talking—

If I can keep him talking—

At least, while he's talking—

We won't be—

"Nan?" he says, looking very puzzled.

He has no idea where I'm coming from.

"What about her?" he asks me.

"Everything."

"Huh?" he says.

"I mean everything you want to tell."

"About my mother?" he asks.

"I just thought . . ." I shrug—because I'm not exactly sure what I just thought yet.

"Funny," he says, "I was thinking. Yesterday, I guess. I was wondering what she'd think about you. You know. About us."

"What do you think? She'd think, I mean?"

"Well . . ." he says.

I've got him really thinking about it now. And so, leaving the door open, I move across the room and, softly, I sit down on the couch beside him.

"Nan'd probably like you a lot," he says. "Once she got over being jealous, that is."

"Jealous?"

He laughs.

"Yeah," he says. "She's always had a thing about the 'other women' in my life. Especially the couple I got serious about. Back as far as I can remember."

"Was she jealous of . . . I don't know her name. But you mentioned her once. At a rehearsal. In the warehouse."

I see him clouding over, like he did the first time he mentioned her.

"Jennifer," he says.

"If you don't want to—"

"She, uh . . . We were sort of going out," he says. "No. We were supposed to be going together. She was wearing my ring. Jennifer was real pretty. Delicate. Like a doll. And real nice . . . At least, she was with me. . . . With everybody else in Greater Atlanta, she was . . ."

He shakes his head, remembering.

"She didn't care," he says. "As long as it wasn't me. She didn't want me thinking she wasn't as nice as I thought she was. It was me she was thinking of, see . . .

"When I found out about . . . you can't mess around with everybody but one person in a band and not have that one person find out about it. . . ! When I first found out, I thought I ought to take her out just one more time. I thought I ought to take her out and take for myself what everybody else was being given."

"Michael!"

"That's how crazy it made me."

"But you didn't—"

"No," he says. "It didn't make me crazy enough to do it. Just to think about it. Crazy enough, I guess."

"Were you in love with her?"

"I thought I was," he admits.

"Did it make Nan jealous?"

"Huh?"

119

"Nan," I remind him.

"Oh," he laughs, happy to change the subject. "Yeah. I guess. I guess, me—you know—getting serious about somebody, anybody—I guess that's always made ol' Nan feel her age."

"How old is ol' Nan?"

"Thirty-six or thirty-seven," he laughs. "But she doesn't like to feel it. Or even think about it, if you don't mind. . . .

"Especially now," he says. "Now that Nan's 'liberated' from my dad and taking classes at Emory. I bet—even at her 'advanced age'—there's nothing she likes better than walking by a bunch of guys and hearing the click of their eyeballs as she passes.

"But even so," he says, smiling up at me from the couch, "I imagine she'd like you. Quite a lot."

"Why do you think?"

"Because I do," he says, reaching up to brush the hair away from my eyes.

"Michael—"

"I really do love you, Jess."

"Oh, Michael . . ."

Outside The Jessie Walters Motel, the sign flashes—

VACANCY

VACANCY

The Other Jessie's back in town!
"Come 'ere . . ."
Like a dream—
Slow.
Gentle.
Irresistible.
His eyes dancing with delight as she leans down to him.

120

Slowly . . . slowly.
Gently . . . gently.
In the darkness . . .
The sweet scuffing of his beard.
The slippery deliciousness of his mouth.
The soft urgency of his hands on her hips.
Moving her over him.
Guiding her to him.
"Michael . . ."
"Shhh . . ."
The tingling rush of air across her breasts.
"Mich—"
"Mm . . ."
"Mm . . ."
"Jess . . ."
The sweet chafing of his chest against her breasts.
"Jess . . . Oh, Jess . . ."
The rub and thrust and shudder of him.
"Oh . . . Oh! . . . Oooooohhh!"

As he falls away from me, I can taste my tears.

"I'm sorry," he gasps, turning away.

"I'm—" I can feel the sobs jumping in my throat. "I'm . . . sorry, too," I tell him.

And I turn away from him.

Beside me, I can hear him, fighting to catch his breath.

"Michael . . .?"

"Mm . . ."

"What are we going to do?"

"I don't know," he says.

"We can't keep . . ."

"No," he says. "We can't."

I can't hold it back anymore. The sobs. They come pouring out of me.

"What are we going to do?"

He takes me in his arms.

Holds me.

121

Comforts me.
"It's okay, honey. It's okay."
But I know he doesn't mean it.
He can't mean it.
It can't go on like this.
Not for long.
It has to end.
One way or another.

Thirty-two

Just when I was looking for something to take my mind off things, school's over.

Today—Friday—is the last half-day of the school year.

It isn't much like a regular school day.

What you do, mainly, is go around from class to class, turning in your textbooks and saying good-bye to your teachers.

Then, around eleven o'clock, everybody files into the school auditorium for an assembly that begins with the principal giving out prizes for a bunch of things you never knew they gave out prizes for—like for having the best attendance record or the neatest penmanship or making the most significant contribution to the audio-visual arts program—things like that.

Then, when that's over, it's time for the traditional Moving-Up Ceremony—where everybody gets a chance to move up a few rows, into the seats where the class ahead of you has been sitting all year, and the graduating class climbs up on the stage and everybody applauds everybody.

Then, we all sing the school song—

> . . . *When we're old and gray*
> *A million miles away*
> *We'll remember all our lives*
> *Our days at JFK.*

And then, it's over.

After nine long months, school's out and summer's in.

Everybody whoops and shouts and does their best to drown out the principal, who's at the microphone, trying to remind us that we're all "ladies and gentlemen" and "JFK's ambassadors to the world at large."

Us ambassadors don't do JFK's reputation a lot of good, the way we take over the bus into Hackensack.

It's close to a riot—and one I'm glad to get free of, when I finally squirm off the bus at the stop closest to The Eddie Nova Guitar Institute.

As always, my lesson with Michael is like a vacation on a tropical island—a million miles away from everything, quiet and calm, sweet and serene.

And even the ride home is like that—talking with Michael about Mr. E's and their layout and their light and sound setup. "Disco plumbing," Michael calls it.

At the curb in front of my house, I kiss Michael good-bye and promise him I'll be all ready for Mr. E's when he comes to pick me up, tomorrow, at seven sharp.

Then—feeling a little better about things than maybe I should—I head inside the house.

Over dinner—Arabian lamb patties called kufta kebab—the family discusses this and that.

I join in, but my mind is on Michael and tomorrow night.

Then, when the dishes have been cleared and everybody's settling down for a second cup of coffee, Bob says, "Okay. It's time."

"Time for what?" I ask him.

"Your birthday present!" he beams.

"My birthday's Sunday. The fourteenth," I remind him. "Today's Friday. The twelfth."

"I know," says Bob. "But this won't keep."

Something's up!

I know it!

All of a sudden!

It's been an okay day—the last day of school, the lesson with Michael, home for dinner, everything, but—

All of a sudden it feels like it's Friday the thirteenth!

"We've had a stroke of luck," says Bob, all bright and cheerful. "Sometimes, you get lucky. And this is one of those times."

"We've won the State Lottery?" I guess.

"Kind of," says Bob, and then—going into his television-game-show routine—he announces, "What we've won, for all of us—and it's your birthday present, kiddo, from Lois and me—what we've won is nothing less than a no-expenses-paid but summer-long vacation in a charming lakeside cottage nestled—just a few short hours away—in the cool comfort of the Catskill Mountains, upstate, in beautiful White Lake, New York!"

Incredible!

"We never go away in the summer!" I tell him.

Unbelievable!

"We never did," Bob confesses with a smile. "Because we never could. But now we can!"

"How can we?"

"A man at work," Lois explains. "A teacher. He and his wife just split up. After twenty-four years. Anyway, they always spent their summers together in White Lake. But now that they're not together anymore, I guess neither one of them wants to, you know, be reminded. And I guess Arnold could use the money."

125

"Which," says Bob, "we just happen to have. Enough of. Just about. With the unused vacation-pay I've been building up."

"It sounds lovely," says Lois.

"Esther can have a garden," says Bob. "A real garden—flowers, vegetables, everything. And your mother will have all kinds of room to paint and walk in the woods, and great views everywhere she looks. And you . . ."

"There's lots of kids up there in the summer," says Lois. "And swimming and boating and horseback riding, movies . . ."

"Everything but Michael," I tell myself. "That's what this is all about."

"Great news, huh?" says Bob, smiling like a man expecting a great big thanks.

"Can I be excused?" I answer.

But I'm not waiting for permission.

I'm on my feet and heading for the door.

As I pass Bob's chair, he says, "We leave Monday."

"No," I think.

"Monday?" I ask him.

I can't believe my ears!

"All of us," Bob nods. "Together."

I just look at him.

And then I look at Lois.

My parents and friends.

The people who love me.

Care about me.

"Thanks a lot," I say. "Both of you."

I say it angrily. And I turn and march out of the dining room, heading for my room, upstairs.

As my foot hits the first step, I hear Bob call from the dining room.

"You're welcome," he calls.

And I can hear the determination in his voice.

I don't slam the door when I get to my room. I just close it.

I don't throw myself onto my bed and burst into tears.

I lie down on my back, eyes dry and open wide.

"Perfect!" I think. "Everything doesn't work out just perfectly."

It makes me laugh.

Honestly.

There's something about life's dirty jokes I can't resist.

Sometimes.

Like now.

"Happy birthday!" I wish myself. "And—oh!—by the way—be sure and say good-bye to Michael for me!"

That makes me laugh, too.

A dry little laugh.

I know there's no way I can convince everybody to give up their bargain-rate dream cottage in the Catskills.

I know there's no way they'll let me stay in Englewood.

Alone.

All summer long.

With Michael around.

That's the whole point, isn't it?

And there's nothing I can do about it, can I?

But say good-bye to Michael.

And know it may be good-bye forever.

And laugh, of course.

Through my tears.

Thirty–three

Merry Christmas!

I know. It's June. June the thirteenth, to be exact. Saturday, June the thirteenth.

I am thirteen years and three hundred and sixty-four days old. Tomorrow, it's "Happy Birthday!" But today, I'm thinking, "Merry Christmas!"

"Merry Christmas, Michael. . . . How are things in Ann Arbor? . . . Great! . . . And how was your summer in Englewood? . . . Great! . . . Hmmm? . . . Oh, sorry. Jessie. Jessie Walters. From The Eddie Nova Guitar Institute. Right . . . Good to see you again. . . . Oh! I didn't—Nice to meet you, Darlene. . . . Well, I guess I should be—Excuse me."

I thought I'd tell Michael about White Lake tonight, at the house, when he picked me up.

But I didn't.

Then I thought, maybe on the way to Mr. E's.

But I didn't.

I'm waiting for the right moment.
Or else I'm chicken.
I'm chicken.
Let's face it.
"Do I have to?"
"Yes."
"Nuts!"
"Anyway . . ."
The thing is, telling Michael that tonight may be our last night together until God knows when, or where or how—

Telling Michael that, starting Monday, he can find me just a few short hours away, in beautiful White Lake—

Well—

That feels so much like saying good-bye, saying good-bye for maybe ever—

I just can't!
"You have to!"
"I know."
"Now!"
"Right."

"That's him!" says Mark, bopping into the dressing room, backstage at Mr. E's.

"You sure?" says Michael.

"Yup," says Mark. "I'm sure, and he's Shore."

"Har! Har!" says Lenny.

"Sandy Shore?" asks Michael. He can't quite believe it.

But Mark nods his head.

"Sounds like a summer resort," says Arnie.

"Har! Har!" says Emily.

"Rock and roll!" Michael shouts, grinning from ear to ear and holding his hand out—palm up—to Mark.

"Rock and roll!" shouts Mark, giving Michael five.

Slap!
Slap!

129

"Rock and roll!"

Slap!

Slap!

Michael goes all around the room until—finally—he gets to me.

"Rock and roll," he smiles.

And he kisses me.

"Rock and roll," I smile.

And I kiss him.

For luck.

And then I turn and head out the door—leaving them alone to get ready, going out front to join the crowd and telling myself, "No. That definitely wasn't the right moment to tell Michael about White Lake."

Because Sandy Shore isn't a summer resort like White Lake.

Sandy Shore is a manager.

Which means his business is discovering bands that nobody's ever heard of and signing them to contracts and booking them into clubs and, generally, putting them on the road to becoming chart-busting, heart-stopping, groupie-guzzling supergroups.

Sandy Shore discovered The Parasites and The Heathens and Fast Freddie and quite a few other bands that I probably should have heard of. Even though I haven't.

I guess it takes time.

But anyway, somebody thought they'd spotted Sandy Shore sitting out front at Mr. E's. And Mark remembered seeing Sandy Shore's picture in *Billboard*. So Michael sent him out front to check it out.

And the rest—as they say—is history.

Or about to be.

I hope.

Out front, there's this table that Michael's got reserved for friends of The Skye Band. It's kind of like a

130

Skye Band Auxiliary, made up mostly of everybody's dates—including Karen, the hippy-dippy redhead, who's with Arnie.

When I say "hello" and join them, they're busy trying not to listen to one of the other two bands that's on the bill with The Skye Band.

The band's called The Ugly Drunks and—if you ask me—they're probably both.

On the other hand, since they aren't actually shrinking the audience for The Skye Band—nobody's actually getting up and walking out on them—and since any halfway decent band—or even a car crash—would sound fabulous after listening to these guys for a while, The Ugly Drunks are okay with me.

As they grunt and howl and make their instruments sound like amplified pots and pans, I look around the room, trying to spot Sandy Shore.

But Mr. E's is packed, and I don't know what Sandy Shore looks like, and even if I did, it's so dark in here, I probably wouldn't recognize my own mother if I saw her.

Peace!

At last.

The Ugly Drunks have apparently decided to call off their demonstration against music.

With everybody else at the table, I join the crowd in giving The Ugly Drunks our—all things considered—generous applause.

I hardly notice, but as we're clapping and laughing and whistling, this dapper little man slips into the empty chair beside me.

"Mind?" he says.

"No," I tell him.

With him already seated beside me, it's a little too late to mind.

Holding his hand out to me, he says, "Sandy Shore."

"Himself!" I think.

But I'm cool.

I reach out and take his hand and shake it and say, "Uh . . . Jessie Walters."

He smiles and says, "Drink?"

I've got the answer to that one, too.

"Uh . . ."

He laughs.

Not at me, exactly. More with me.

"Yeah," he says, giving me a wink. "I'm on the wagon myself."

I send him a smile.

But he's not there to receive it.

I mean, he's still there—sitting in the chair right next to me—but I don't have his attention anymore.

What's more interesting to him than me is the technical crew—Mr. E's has its own—breaking down The Ugly Drunk's equipment and setting up The Skye Band's.

What's so interesting about these guys stumbling around the stage, I can't tell you.

But then, I'm not Sandy Shore.

"Ladies and gentle— . . . Mr. E's . . ."

The Skye Band's equipment is set up.

". . . the rock capital of northern New Jersey . . ."

The Skye Band is on stage, tuned and ready.

"Is proud to present—for the first time on our stage—Give a big welcome to The Skye Band!"

And they do.

Not just The Skye Band Auxiliary, but everybody.

We clap and shout and cheer as Michael and the band rip into "Better Than It's Ever Been Before."

I wanna take y'—take y' home with me.
And when I show y'—how it's s'posed to be.
You'll close your eyes and grin.

132

You'll know the place you're in—
It's better than it's ever been before . . .

It's the first song I ever saw Michael sing. It was so
wonderful then, I fell in love with him right on the spot.

But tonight—with all the rehearsals and perfor-
mances behind them, with Sandy Shore sitting out
front, watching them—The Skye Band storms into "It's
Better Than It's Ever Been Before," and it *is* better
than it's ever been before.

Ten times better!

Right from the start, The Skye Band comes out
sky-high and climbing.

And now, moment by moment, you can feel them—
feeding off one another, feeding off the crowd—
building higher and higher.

Hear the music
Let it lift you off the floor.
Till there's nothin' but the music, anymore.
Forget about the world outside the door.
It's better than it's ever been before . . .

Around the room, I can see the crowd, rocking with
them, rolling with them, rooting them home.

But out of the corner of my eye, I check out the main
attraction—

I watch Sandy Shore watching the band.

Is he loving them?

Is he hating them?

Beats me!

Because what Sandy Shore does while Michael and
The Skye Band are doing what they're doing—which is
simply sensational—is—

He stares at them.

He kind of purses his lips together.

He nods his head up and down, very slightly—but
never in rhythm with the tune.

And—every now and then—he bows his head and closes his eyes and cups his hand around his right ear.

At the end of the song, while the crowd is going crazy, loving Michael and the band—he claps his hands.

Four or five times.

And—as he does—he looks all around the room.

As if he was looking for a waitress.

Or a friend.

Or an exit.

Now, all of this is fascinating in its own way.

I mean, watching this bald little man with his round little belly popping out through the flaps of his double-breasted blue blazer.

Watching him study Michael and the band like a little old pawnbroker, sitting alone in a dark little room, looking through an eyepiece at somebody's maybe-diamond ring.

That's pretty fascinating.

In its own way.

But it's also pretty frustrating.

In its own way.

Because, watching Sandy Shore watching Michael and The Skye Band, I can't tell whether he thinks he's looking at a diamond or a piece of glass.

Not until it's all over.

At the very end.

After Michael and The Skye Band have roared and soared through seven songs and two encores.

The whole crowd gets up on its feet—some people actually climb up on their chairs—and they applaud and cheer and really let it out.

Sandy Shore doesn't get to his feet.

Not right away.

He just sits there, looking at the crowd standing all around him—like a tourist in the city, staring at the tall buildings.

But then, finally, he pulls himself up to his feet and

134

he says to us—everybody at this table Michael's set aside for us—"If you don't mind, I'd like a few seconds alone with the boys. If you don't mind."

Mind?

We're The Skye Band Auxiliary.

We don't mind!

Thirty–four

I am standing with the rest of The Skye Band Auxiliary in this narrow backstage corridor, outside The Skye Band's dressing room.

All of us are waiting for Sandy Shore to finish talking with the band.

We're waiting for the door to open.

We're waiting to congratulate everybody in the band on their terrific performance.

And one of us—me—is still waiting for the right moment—the moment to tell Michael that I've been exiled to White Lake, New York, for the whole summer.

So far, all of the moments have been wrong.

But any moment now—

The dressing-room door opens, and Sandy Shore pops out into the narrow corridor.

"Be in touch," he tells Michael, shaking his hand at the door.

"Thanks," says Michael.

Then, spotting us—me and the rest of The Skye Band Auxiliary, waiting in the corridor—Sandy pats Michael's shoulder and tells us, "Good kid. Real good kid."

With that, Sandy gives Michael a parting wink and then he turns and bustles off down the corridor.

Michael turns to us and—tilting his head toward Sandy—he smiles and says, "Our manager."

"Eeeeehaw!"

Everybody—me and Michael, The Skye Band Auxiliary and the rest of the band, who come pouring out of the dressing room—everybody lets go with a hoot or a howl or a holler or a shout.

And everybody hugs everybody.

And kisses everybody.

"Party!" shouts Mark.

And everybody picks it up.

"Party! Party! Party!"

"My place!" Mark shouts.

"Eeeeehaw!"

"Yo!"

"Rock and roll!"

How's that for a wrong moment to tell Michael about White Lake?

Not bad, huh?

But I let it pass.

Because here comes another one that's just as wrong.

We're riding in Michael's car. Just Michael and me. Moving down the road. Heading for the party at Mark's.

The idea is, we're going to stop in at Mark's house, just long enough for Michael to have a beer and celebrate a little before he takes me home.

That's the idea.

But now, while we're still on the road, Michael starts telling me about Sandy Shore.

He's trying to be cool about the whole thing, but I

137

can see he's having a hard time keeping the smile off his face.

According to Michael, what Sandy Shore has in mind for The Skye Band is becoming their manager and booking them into a bunch of little clubs where vacationing record-company executives hang out when they get sick of their country houses and the country air and their record collections and their old ladies and all the rest of it.

The thing is, any one of these bored record-company executives could get turned on by The Skye Band—especially after the band's been playing together, night after night, getting their music down sharper and tighter—and any one of these bored record-company executives could sign The Skye Band to a record contract and start them on their way up the ladder.

Michael says he's not all that sure he wants to start climbing up Sandy Shore's ladder just yet.

But he's happy that, at least, Sandy's offering him the chance. And even if he doesn't want to climb Sandy's ladder, just having him as a manager and getting booked into these better clubs means he'll be making more money this summer than he'd figured on.

Michael says—considering the opportunity Sandy Shore's offering them—he felt a little shamefaced, asking Sandy how much the band would actually get paid for playing in these little clubs.

But he was thinking about money for Michigan and so he asked.

Sandy Shore smiled at Michael and said, "Oh, about twenty-five percent more than you get in a place like this."

Which sounded pretty good.

Until Sandy Shore laughed and said, "But that's *my* cut!"

Which turned out to be a joke.

Michael figured if everything worked out, Sandy Shore could earn him an extra five thousand dollars this summer.

He also figured—besides the money—getting a manager and getting booked into all these clubs with the bored record-company executives was a pretty good score, especially after only one night's work at Mr. E's.

And when Michael looked around the dressing room, he could see that everybody in the band agreed with him.

And so Michael told Sandy, yes, The Skye Band would be happy to have him as their manager.

And Sandy said, if Michael would shake his hand to seal the bargain, he'd get busy right away, digging up a place for The Skye Band to play next weekend.

So Michael looked around the room again, and everybody nodded their heads and Michael shook Sandy's hand.

And now Michael can't hold it back anymore.

Positively glowing with happiness, he looks over at me and shouts, "Whoooooooeee!"

I laugh and push over closer to him and tell him how wonderful I think it all is and how happy I am for him.

But, getting serious all at once, Michael tells me, "There is a hitch, though."

I brace myself.

"These little clubs Sandy wants us to play in. The ones where the record guys hang out. They're not just in New Jersey. They're all over the Northeast—New York, Pennsylvania, Vermont, Massachusetts. . . . We'll be on the road most of the summer. Traveling from state to state. Going from club to club."

"You mean," I ask him, "you won't be spending a lot of time around Englewood this summer?"

Looking real sad and real sorry, Michael says, "Hardly any."

And I break up.

Laughing.

At first.

But then, I start crying.

Bawling.

Isn't it incredible?

Michael's apologizing to me.

He's upset about my crying.

And he thinks I'm crying because he's running out on me.

But I'm crying because he's running out on me *and* because I'm running out on him.

Both.

At once.

Incredible!

But I'm not being fair.

"It doesn't matter," I tell Michael. "I'm not going to be here, either."

"All summer?" he says.

I laugh.

I'm still crying but I'm laughing too.

"I'll be upstate, in White Lake, New York," I tell him.

He looks over at me.

For what seems like a long time.

Just letting it sink in.

How really incredible it is.

What's happened to us.

He looks back at the road.

He doesn't say anything for a second.

But then, he looks up in his rearview mirror and out his window at the mirror on the side of his door.

And he swerves the wagon into a U-turn—making it fast and tight.

And he heads us back the way we came.

140

For the last half hour now, I've been fourteen years old.

Thank you.

Happy birthday to you, too.

The thing is—if things keep going like this—by the time I'm fifteen, I'll be a hundred and twenty.

Thirty–five

Michael lives with his father in one of those fancy, high-rise apartment buildings that towers over Route 4 and looks down on the commuter traffic that snakes into the city every morning and slinks home from the city every night.

Michael's father commutes to the city.

But he snakes more than he slinks.

He doesn't get home every night.

They keep him busy at the office is what he tells Michael.

But Michael's noticed that they keep his father especially busy at the office on weekends—when the office is closed.

Michael's father almost never comes home on weekends.

So Michael's father isn't here.

In Michael's apartment.

Nobody's here.

Except Michael and me.

Just the two of us.

Nobody else.

But I'm not nervous.

I'm petrified!

"It's nice," I tell Michael.

Commenting on his living room.

Just for something to say.

And to see if my jaw's working.

"Come on," says Michael, holding out his hand for me to take.

"Where?"

He smiles.

"My room . . ."

"Uh . . ."

"I want you to see it," he says.

And reaching his hand out to me again, he says, "Come on."

I can't!

I can't go through with this!

"Michael," I plead.

Taking his hand, I pull it back, behind my waist—so now his arm is wrapped around me.

And now I wrap my free arm around him and—holding him close—I press my cheek against his chest and close my eyes.

I can't go through with it!

I can't!

Michael holds me.

Hugs me.

Strokes my hair.

"Whatever happens . . ." he says.

I open my eyes and look up at him.

Looking down into my eyes, he says, "We go on."

"Forever?" I ask him.

"And then some," he nods.

And he leans down.

And kisses me.

Thirty–six

Walking into Michael's room is like walking into another world.

It's dark and warm.

Soft music is playing.

And out Michael's window, the lights of New York City are twinkling through a hazy fog of midnight blue.

Michael's desk—with its clothes-covered chair—stands by the window.

Michael's six guitar cases sit in the corner, lined up like horses outside a Western saloon.

Against the wall—behind a coffee table littered with magazines—lies Michael's narrow bed.

Otherwise, the room is bare.

Except for Michael.

And me.

Outside The Jessie Walters Motel, the sign flashes—

VACANCY

VACANCY

VACANCY

But no one stands on the sidewalk, looking up at the sign.

It continues flashing.

And up and down the street, the sidewalk stretches empty into the echoing night.

Funny.

How *The Other Jessie* put me here, and—now when I need her—she's nowhere in sight!

Funny.

How *The Other Jessie* left me here—me, of all people—to finish up what *she* started!

"Funny," I think.

"Relax," Michael whispers.

But how can I?

How can I relax when we're lying together on Michael's bed?

When Michael's kissing me?

And undressing me?

And looking at me?

And touching me?

How can I?

"Easy," says Michael.

"I'm trying," I tell him.

"Don't," he whispers. "Don't try. Just relax and let it happen. I'll do the rest."

"I'll try."

He smiles at me.

And leans down.

And kisses me.

Long and deep and—oh, so tenderly.

145

And I try—
To lose myself in his kiss—
To surrender myself to him—
To this!
I try—
To find *her* in his kiss—
To surrender myself to *her*—
To this!
But I can't lose myself!
And I can't find *her!*
But it doesn't matter now.
It's too late.
Because Michael's found me!
And—Oh!—"Ow!"
"Sorry," he gasps.
But he doesn't stop.
He can't stop.
And I can't get started.
Not until—
Just when I think I might—
"Oh, God! Jess! . . . So good! . . . You feel so—Oh!
. . . Honey! . . . I love you so much! . . . If you
only—Oh! . . . So much! . . . Oh, Jess! . . . Now! . . .
Now, Jess! . . . So—Oh! Ooo! Oooooohhh . . ."
It's over.
Just like that.
The whole clumsy, embarrassing, stupid, stupid,
stupid thing is over.
BANG.
Just like that.

Thirty-seven

After—

Michael pulls the blanket up around us and—as he tells me how everything is going to work out fine for us and how we'll go on and on, forever and ever—I lie in his arms, listening and thinking.

You'd imagine that making love was really fabulous, wouldn't you?

I mean, you'd expect it to be sensational, wouldn't you?

Because of how they say it is in songs and in books?

And how they show you it is on television and in the movies?

I mean, if I asked you what making love was like—if you really thought about it—wouldn't you say making love was something like watching *a slow cascade of softly tumbling images, a rhapsody of suntanned bodies, floating in a linen-white cloud over a sea of swelling music and the muted sound of sighs and sobs and laughter?*

Or would you say that making love was painful and clumsy and embarrassing and stupid?

Would you say both?

Would you say neither?

You'd go for the slow cascade, right?

For the suntanned bodies and the linen-white clouds and all the rest?

Sure, you would.

I mean, that's what everybody tells you it's like.

So what else are you supposed to think?

It's like Santa Claus.

Everybody told you about him, too, didn't they?

And remember how you felt when you found out?

Like the entire world—and especially the people you loved best and trusted most—like everybody had been playing this elaborate and cruel joke on you?

Like they'd been making a fool of you?

Like, all along, they'd been laughing at you?

Laughing behind your back?

Well, that's what I feel like right now.

Like they fooled me again.

Like, here I am, fourteen years old and finding out all over again that there's no Santa Claus.

"Merry Christmas, Jessie!"

"Happy birthday, Jessie!"

"April Fool, Jessie!"

I feel like such a jerk.

And Michael.

How do you suppose he feels?

Now—

After—

It couldn't have been much fun for him, either.

I couldn't have been much fun.

I mean, I was supposed to say, "Wow!" wasn't I?

But I said "Ow!" didn't I?

That couldn't have been much fun for Michael, could it?

I mean, it couldn't have been the kind of fun that

anybody would come running back for more of, could it?

I mean, you wouldn't hold your breath until the next time Michael and I make love, would you?

"Would you like that?"

"Huh?"

"If I could get up to White Lake after the weekend?"

"You think you could?"

"I don't see why not," he says. "It's not that far. I could probably get up and back the same day."

"Yeah."

"It's just a matter of figuring out what day we're going to have off, is all."

"Uh-huh."

"We've got to have a day off. It's just a matter of when. . . . Jess?"

"Mmm."

"You ready for your birthday present?"

"You mean . . . that . . . wasn't it?"

"Huh?" he says.

But then, he gets it.

And laughs.

And hugs me.

"Nope," he says, and—as he says it—he lifts the blanket and slides out from under it and slips into his jeans.

As he stands and walks over to the corner where he keeps his guitars, I scoop my blouse and my slacks and things off the floor and pull them under the blanket and start getting dressed.

"Actually," he says—he's kneeling over his guitars, and his back is to me—"what I really wanted to give you isn't ready, yet."

He picks out a guitar and starts unpacking it from its case.

"But at least I can give you a peek at how it's shaping up," he says.

The last time I remember getting dressed under a

blanket was at this camp I went to one summer. It was so cold when they woke you at six in the morning—with a bugle playing "Reveille" over a scratchy loudspeaker—you'd stack your clothes up next to your bed at night, so you wouldn't have to greet the icy dawn wearing nothing but your birthday suit.

"I don't know why it's giving me so much trouble," says Michael, still kneeling in the corner with his guitars. "Maybe I'm trying too hard to get it just right."

He gets to his feet now and—with his back still turned to me—he starts tuning the guitar he's picked out.

"You okay?" he asks.

"I'm dressed," I tell him, "if that's what you mean."

"Yeah," he says, turning to me with a smile.

"You're beautiful," he says.

I don't feel beautiful.

I feel—

Suddenly, I feel—

Very self-conscious.

Like there's a caption under me—

Like under a picture in a magazine—

JESSIE WALTERS,
THE FAMOUS FORMER VIRGIN.

It's like—
Just looking at me—
Anybody could see!
They could see—
Right off the bat—
What I've just done.
What I'm not, anymore.
What I'll never be again.
They could see.
I know it!
Especially Lois.
And Bob.

150

And Grandma.

What'll they think?

What can I do?

Where can I go?

Where can I hide?

"Well," says Michael, dropping onto the bed beside me, "here's what I've got so far, anyway."

And he begins playing—the song he's been working on—the one that's got something to do with me—the one that's going to be a bear if he ever gets it down—the one that's pretty and sad and a little strange—like me.

And I watch him sitting there, strumming, wearing nothing but his jeans and his guitar and his smile.

And I listen to his song—the song he wanted to give me for my birthday.

And it's so pretty, so haunting, so gentle, so sure—

And he's so sweet and sincere, playing the song so easy and fine—

And it could have been so nice—

Me and Michael—

Making love—

Going on and on—

Forever and ever—

I can't help but cry.

And when he finishes, when he's played as much of the song as he's written, I am still crying.

"That's about as much as I've got, so far," he says, apologizing to me because he doesn't have more.

"It's beautiful, Michael."

He smiles.

Shyly.

"I told you it had something to do with you," he says.

"Thank you."

"But that's not your present," he says, "since it isn't finished yet."

"This is your present," he says.

And he hands me his guitar.

151

"Oh, Michael," I tell him, shaking my head, "I couldn't."

"It's old," he says, "the oldest one I've still got hold of. It's knocked around some and got banged up a little, but it still plays good. And it's a whole lot better than what you're used to."

"Michael . . ."

"I want you to have it, Jess."

I take his guitar and I tell him, "Thank you."

And—leaning over my new guitar—I kiss him.

He smiles.

"Will you take me home now?" I ask him.

"Do you love me?" he says.

"With all my heart."

"Happy birthday, Jess."

He kisses me.

"Merry Christmas, Michael."

"Huh?"

"Just a joke," I tell him, "a stupid joke."

Thirty–eight

I should have thought about it before.

But I didn't.

Or maybe I did.

But if I did think about it, I thought about it just long
enough to tell myself not to think about it.

Probably because I thought that thinking about it
would ruin everything.

So, either way, you could say I didn't really think
about it before.

Although I know I should have.

I thought about it after, though.

Right after.

I mean, you have to.

If you make love, you have to think about getting
pregnant.

Especially if nobody was exactly planning on making
love and nobody did anything about not getting pregnant.

You really have to think about it.

About being pregnant.

And telling your mother.

And the two of you—you and your mother—going to a doctor to find out for sure.

And having him say—

"Yes, you're pregnant."

And—

"What would you like to do about it?"

"Nothing."

"I'm afraid it's a little late for that."

"Late?"

"You're going to have to spend the next nine months carrying—and then giving birth to—a fine, healthy baby. Or else, sometime in the next few weeks, you're going to have to get rid of it. There's no third choice. Not that I know of."

"Mom!"

I thought about it, all right.

Right after, and all the way home.

I thought maybe I should say something to Michael about it.

And then, I thought maybe I shouldn't.

Because maybe I wasn't.

Pregnant, I mean.

"And anyway," I thought, "if I am—if I am pregnant—telling Michael can wait—until after next weekend—when he comes to see me—at White Lake."

"I can tell him then—if I am—that I am—pregnant."

So I didn't say anything.

Except for telling Michael that I loved him.

Which I do.

And good night.

Which it wasn't.

Because I was thinking about it.

And even after I got into the house and got upstairs without waking anyone—

154

And even after I took off all my clothes and stood, looking at myself in the mirror, trying to see if anything showed—

And even after I got into bed and turned out the light and closed my eyes—

I thought about it.

Thirty–nine

What a night.

One minute, I'm lying there with all these thoughts and pictures racing around in my head.

And then, the next thing I know, all these people I know are all upset about this girl who's in some kind of trouble.

I'm upset, too.

I don't know why, exactly.

But it begins to dawn on me—the trouble this girl is in.

She's pregnant.

And who this girl in trouble is.

She's me.

But just when I'm about to figure it all out, everything changes.

It goes into a tailspin.

And suddenly, I'm a prisoner in a Horror Show!

A Horror Show with a Hair-Raising Conclusion that I don't want to stick around for.

Fighting with all my might, I wrench myself out of it.

I wake myself up.

I lie in the darkness of my room, sweating and trying to catch my breath.

And then, all these thoughts and pictures start racing around in my head again.

And then, the next thing I know, all these people I know are all upset about this girl who's in some kind of trouble again.

Etcetera.

And so forth.

All night and all morning long.

Until I finally haul myself out of bed.

And now—it must be way past noon—I'm standing and looking at this wasted, puffy-eyed, one-hundred-forty-year-old girl who is staring out at me from the mirror on top of my dresser.

"Still dreaming," I think. "Shake yourself out of it."

I look the one-hundred-forty-year-old girl right in the eye and I tell her, "You're pregnant!"

She doesn't blink.

"Serves you right!" I tell her.

We laugh.

A sad laugh.

Me and her.

Then me alone.

I'm awake.

And I'm not pregnant.

I can't be pregnant until I miss my period—which isn't due until Wednesday or so.

And even then—even if by Friday or so, I still haven't gotten my period—I can't be pregnant until a doctor says I am.

So I'm not pregnant.

At least, I don't know I'm pregnant.

Which is practically the same thing.

I tell myself.

And I almost believe it.

157

For a second.

Long enough to pull on my clothes and slump down to the kitchen and pour myself a cup of coffee.

Out the kitchen window, I can see Lois working with Grandma, getting the backyard ready for a summer of inattention.

I don't want to talk to Lois.

Not to her or Grandma or Bob or even Michael.

I'm afraid if I talk to anybody—if anybody even says, "How are you?" to me—I'll burst into tears, scream "Help! I'm pregnant!" and collapse into their arms.

That's what I'm afraid of.

So—standing by the window, sipping my coffee—I take a Vow of Silence.

Until I get hold of myself, I'm not talking to anybody.

Not Lois.

Not Grandma.

Not Bob.

Not even Michael.

I wonder if he called.

I rap on the window.

Right away, outside in the backyard, Lois looks up at me from a bush she's mulching. She smiles and waves at me and motions for me to come outside.

I congratulate myself on how well I've done, keeping my Vow of Silence.

I take a deep breath. I walk to the back door. I walk out onto the back landing—that's as far as I'll go—and I say, "'Morning!" as brightly as I can.

"'Morning?" asks Grandma, giving the hedges a smart clip. "The day's half over!"

"Home late?" Lois smiles.

"Yeah," I confess, hoping that's the last of her questions about last night.

"Michael called," she says.

"Oh?"

"Around eleven."

"Oh."

"He said he'd call back."

"Great."

"Did you have breakfast?"

"I'm not hungry."

"You'd better eat anyway. There's lots of hard work to be done if we're going to get out of here tomorrow."

"Okay," I tell her, and I turn and start heading back into the house.

That's when I hear the doorbell.

"Doorbell!" Lois calls.

"I'll get it," I tell her and—instead of going back through the house—I walk down the steps and follow the driveway out to the front porch.

"Caroline!"

She's standing at the front door.

"What happened to you?" she demands.

"She knows!" I think. *"She can tell! Just looking at me, she can tell!"*

Denying everything, I tell her, "Nothing."

"Nothing! You were supposed to meet me! At The Station! Remember? Our farewell lunch?"

I was!

"Oh, Caroline . . . !"

I said I would. Yesterday, on the phone.

I remembered, too.

Until last night.

Does sex affect your memory?

"Goodbye!" she says, and she turns and she starts coming down the steps, heading for the sidewalk.

But I cut her off at the bottom of the steps.

"Hey! I'm sorry," I tell her.

"I'll bet!" she fumes.

"I just woke up," I explain.

"Really?" she says, looking interested all of a sudden.

159

"Were you out late with Michael?"

I don't want to talk to Caroline.

Even though she wouldn't know what to ask.

I don't want to talk to her because I might burst out in tears and scream, "Help! I'm pregnant!" etc.

But I can't send her away, either.

Not after I've just stood her up.

"Come on in," I tell her.

She thinks about it.

"I'm sorry, Caroline."

She accepts it.

In partial payment.

As I lead her up the stairs and into the house, she tells me, "It was embarrassing. Being at The Station. Alone. Waiting for somebody who never showed up."

"Was it crowded?" I ask her, heading for the kitchen and hoping to change the subject on the way.

"Enough!" she says.

Arriving in the kitchen, I tell her, "I'm really sorry."

"What time did you get home last night?" she asks. "What did you do?"

"Want some coffee?"

"Yuk!"

"Milk?"

"What did you do, Jessie?"

"Coke?"

"Jessie!"

"Guess what?" I spring it at her, all excited. "Michael's got a manager!"

"Yeah?" she says, picking up my excitement and settling into a chair at the kitchen table. "What's that?"

I figure, one way to avoid talking to people is to talk *at* them—a mile a minute, so they can't get a word in edgewise.

So I start explaining the whole thing to Caroline, adding all kinds of details that I make up as I go along.

But it isn't long before Caroline sees through my Motormouth Marathon.

I can see her getting impatient with all my talk about managers and bookings and things.

I can see her aching to get back to last night and what Michael and I did that made me sleep so late.

"And you should see their record collections!" I tell her.

"Oh," says Lois, barging in the kitchen door, "Caroline! I wondered who it was."

"I just dropped in to say good-bye," Caroline explains. "After Jessie didn't show up for lunch."

"Oh," says Lois, looking confused. "But you're going to visit us at White Lake, aren't you?"

"Jessie invited me," Caroline says. "But I've got a real busy schedule this summer. I'm jumping."

"Oh," says Lois, looking even more confused than she did before.

And the phone rings.

Saved by the bell!

"I'll get it!" I shout, and I beat Lois to the phone.

"Hello?"

"Hi, Jess . . ."

It's Michael!

"How y' doin'?" he says.

"Uh . . . Fine!" I say. "Except I'm here talking to Caroline. And my mother. How are you?"

"Are you all right?" he asks, sounding real sweet and sincere and sympathetic.

"Terrific," I lie. "Hang on, okay?"

"Want me to call back later?" he says.

"Hang on," I tell him.

Cupping my hand over the mouthpiece, I turn to Caroline and—apologizing—I tell her, "It's Michael."

"No kidding," she says, real grumpy. "I've gotta be going, anyway."

As she gets up from the table, I tell her, "No."

"It's okay," she lies, heading for the door. "Have a nice summer."

"Caroline!"

161

"Have a nice summer, Mrs. Walters."

As Caroline marches out of the kitchen, heading for the front door, Lois shoots me an angry look.

"'Bye, Caroline!" I call.

"'Bye," she calls.

The front door closes behind her.

I give Lois a smile, like "See? It's all right!"

But Lois doesn't buy it.

She shakes her head and heads out the back door.

"Don't forget your packing," she reminds me.

"I won't," I assure her.

But she's already out the door and past hearing.

"Michael?"

"What was all that?"

"Nothing," I tell him.

I don't know why I did it!

Why I chased Caroline out when it's Michael I don't want to talk to most!

"You sure you're okay?" he says.

"Help! I'm pregnant!" I think.

"Yeah," I tell him. "Sure. Why shouldn't I be?"

"I want to see you," he says.

"No," I tell him. "I've got all this packing to do. And the backyard and everything. I've got to do my share."

"You can't get out for a half hour?" he says.

"I don't think so."

"I want to say good-bye."

"You just did," I tell him.

"I want to see you when I say good-bye," he says.

"I can't."

"You still love me, Jess?"

"Of course!" I tell him.

"Good," he says. "I'll see you later."

"Mich—!"

But he's hung up already.

And left me with the dial tone.

I plead with it—"Please don't."

But he does.

During dinner.

Dessert, really.

The doorbell rings.

"It's Michael," I announce, getting up from the table.

"You haven't finished packing," Lois reminds me.

"I'm not going anywhere," I tell her, heading for the door.

"Hi," he says.

He is beautiful.

I do love him.

If only—!

"Can you come out? Or do I have to come in?"

"Mom!" I call. "I'll be out on the front porch for a second."

I step out on the porch and close the door behind me.

It's not really a porch—our front porch. It's just this platform with no place to sit except for this skinny iron railing that runs around it.

So that's where we sit, Michael and I, perched side by side on the skinny iron railing.

"I can't stay long," I warn him.

"That's okay," he says. "I just wanted to see you. And make sure you're okay."

"What do you think?" I ask him, showing him my dramatic profile and my Cover-girl smile.

But he's not looking at me.

He's studying his hands, resting in his lap.

"Sometimes," he says, "at least for girls, anyway— sometimes, the first time—I guess it's—I don't know— scary, I guess."

"I'm okay," I tell him.

"You sure?" he says, looking at me, looking into my eyes.

"You coming to White Lake?"

"Yeah," he says. "Sure."

"Will you call me and tell me when?" I ask him.

"Sure," he says.

"But you don't know my number," I remind him.

"Not yet," he smiles. "Give it to me."

"I don't know it, either."

"Well," he says, "what's the name of the people who own the place?"

"Arnold."

"They got a first name?"

"That *is* their—I mean, it's his—Michael?"

"Yeah?" he says.

"Why don't I call you and give you the number when I get there?"

"I don't know," he jokes. "Why don't you?"

I laugh.

Kind of halfheartedly.

But still—

"Will you be home?" I ask him.

"Tomorrow night?" he says—like he's running over his social calendar in his head.

"Yeah," I tell him.

"You're going to call?" he asks.

"Uh-huh," I nod.

He smiles his wonderful smile at me and looks deep into my eyes.

"I'll be home, Jess," he promises.

And he slips his arm around my waist.

"You're so beautiful," he says.

"Oh, Michael . . ."

"Jess . . ."

He kisses me.

Sweetly.

So sweetly.

So sweetly that it all comes back.

Last night.

Everything.

"Jess," he says.

He wants to kiss me again.

I want to kiss him again, too.

But I don't dare.

"Say good night, Michael."

"Good night, Michael," he says.

"Michael!"

He smiles.

I kiss him.

Quickly.

And I go inside.

Through the screen door, I watch Michael moving down the walk, climbing into his wagon, starting up and driving off.

After he's gone, I close the front door.

"Jess? Don't you want to finish your dessert?" Lois calls from the dining room.

"No," I answer, heading for the stairs. "I've still got some packing to do."

"It'll wait," Bob calls.

"No, thanks," I call.

"I'll eat it all myself!" he warns me.

"Fine," I call.

I walk into my room and close the door behind me.

"I should call Caroline," I remind myself. "I have to ask her to forgive me. For The Station. And the kitchen, when Michael called."

But Caroline would want to know why I'm crying.

And there are so many reasons.

I couldn't begin to tell her.

Forty

Bob is due back from the County Highway Department any time now. He had a few things he wanted to clean up before we took off for White Lake.

It's taken him longer than he planned. It's going on two, and we've already got everything we didn't pack into Bob's car, packed into Lois's car.

Now there's nothing to do but wait for Bob.

That and call Caroline.

Which I've been putting off all morning.

I dial her number.

She answers.

"It's me," I tell her.

"Oh," she says—like she's disappointed to hear it.

"Caroline," I tell her, "I really didn't mean to be . . ."

"Rotten?" she guesses.

"Yeah," I admit. "And rude. And insensitive. And . . ."

"Thoughtless?" she suggests.

"Yeah," I agree.

I wait for her to say something.

She doesn't.

"Will you forgive me?" I ask her.

"You were probably upset," she says. "Leaving Englewood and Michael."

"And my friends," I add.

"Your friends are pretty upset, too!" she reminds me.

"There's only one of them I really care about," I tell her. "That's why I'm calling her and asking her if she could please forgive me before I go."

I hear Bob's car pulling into the driveway.

"When is that?" Caroline asks me.

"Any second now," I tell her.

I hear Bob's car door banging shut.

"Well," she says, "you were pretty awful."

"I know."

"But . . . seeing as you are my best friend . . ."

"Oh, Caroline!"

"I forgive you." She sighs.

"Jessie!"

It's Bob, bellowing to me from the driveway.

"Will you come visit me?" I ask Caroline.

"Just tell me when you want me," she says.

"Jessie!"

Now it's Bob and Lois and Grandma, all together, like a chorus, calling to me.

"Coming!" I shout.

"Sorry," I tell Caroline. "I've got to go."

"Have a real good time, Jess."

"You, too," I tell her. "I'll call you."

"Please," she says.

"Thanks," I tell her.

"'Bye, Jess."

"Thanks, Caroline."

"Jessie!"

"Okay, okay!"

167

I was kind of hoping Bob's car would get totaled this morning.

That Bob would be okay, but his car would be so totaled that—in sympathy—Lois's car would refuse to go to White Lake.

Now or ever.

I was also hoping—even though we said good-bye last night and even though I'm going to talk to him tonight and even though I still don't want to talk to him—I was kind of hoping Michael would call before we left.

But then, I used to hope the first time I made love, it would be fantastic.

I didn't get that one, either.

What I get instead is a chance to spend two or three hours locked in a car with my talkative, curious, concerned father.

It's not something I'm looking forward to.

But Grandma's riding up to White Lake with Lois, in Lois's car.

So I get Bob.

And even though I am not wearing handcuffs, I feel like a dangerous convict being transferred to a maximum security prison.

Because I've been breaking out of my minimum security prison too much.

It's gotten embarrassing for the wardens.

Bob and Lois.

Too embarrassing.

So it's Devil's Island for "Babyface" Jessie Walters.

And throw away the key.

On the other hand, the trip to White Lake isn't half bad.

For one thing, Warden Bob is as happy as a clam—putting the County Highway Department behind him and taking his first summer vacation since he was my age.

For another thing, Warden Bob's picked up a Red Sox-Yankee game on the car radio and—just like a true Bosox fan sitting in Fenway Park, munching on a Fenway Frank and guzzling a 'Gansett—Warden Bob's shouting to his heroes and cheering his team on.

And best of all, now that Warden Bob's taken himself out to the ballgame, I don't have to worry about talking to him or bursting into tears or shouting, "Help! I'm pregnant!"

In fact, it's possible—if the game gets tied up and goes into extra innings—I could ride all the way to White Lake and never have to say a word to Warden Bob.

So—

Even though I don't know I'm not pregnant—

Even though I do know I'm definitely in the process of being separated from Michael—

Even though, when I call Michael tonight, I don't want to talk to him—

Even though, when I see Michael again—*if* I see Michael again—I don't know what I'll do—

The trip up to White Lake is the first chance I've had in a long time to just kick back and try to relax.

So—

Like I said—

It isn't half bad.

In fact, there's something soothing about the sound of the car rushing along the road, and the ballgame droning out from the radio, and Bob chiming in with his yays and boos as the Red Sox fortunes rise and fall.

And there's something relaxing about the sight of the buildings along the sides of the road, shrinking and aging and growing farther apart as we wind from street to road to highway, from interstate to interstate, heading north, away from the city, moving out toward the country.

But the best thing is the greenness—in the lawns that

turn into fields that sprout shrubs—in the saplings that thicken into groves and woods and forests right before your eyes as you move along.

There's something about it.

About all the greenness.

And the sound of a car rushing along the road.

And the ballgame droning out from the radio.

And Warden Bob yaying and booing.

It's like . . . like . . . Mmm . . . I feel so good . . . so tired . . .

"Mind if I take a nap?"

"With the score tied at three-three?"

"Who's winning?" I ask him.

"Good night, kiddo," he says.

"Mmmmmmmmmmmmmmuuuuuuuuuuuuuuuuzzzzz-zzzzzzzzzzzzzzzzzzzzzzzzzzzzzzzzzzzzzzzzzzzzzzzzzzzzzzzzzz-zzzzzzzzzzzzzzzzzzzzzz . . ."

"Yo!!!"

"Wha? . . ."

"Yo! Yaz!!!"

Bob's gone crazy!

"Eight-four! Grand slam! The bottom of the twelfth! Yaz!!! Yo!!!"

"Where are we?"

"Oh," he says, turning to me, "did *you* miss a game!"

"Where are we?"

"Currently," Bob announces, flashing me his game-show host grin, "we are on Lake Road, in the probably unincorporated village of White Lake, New York, not more than three or four telephone poles—I'm losing count because of you—twelve, thirteen—from a mail-box with the name Barnes painted on—There it is!"

Glancing quickly into the rearview mirror—Lois's car is nowhere in sight—Bob whips the car into a sharp left turn that takes us bouncing over a clackety hump of wooden bridge and down a winding gravel road through a tunnel of overhanging trees.

A few death-defying seconds later, we pop out of the tunnel and into a clearing and pull to a stop before a saggy-roofed little house with silvery shingles and touches of white around the windows and on the railings of a wrap-around porch.

A second later, Bob is standing beside the car, his hands on his hips, admiring his silvery dream cottage and, just beyond it, White Lake's sun-dappled waters.

Still half asleep, I haul myself out of the car and stagger over to Bob's side.

He greets me with a smile and—throwing his arm around me—he turns once more to admire the view.

"Fantastic, isn't it?"

"Yeah," I tell him, doing what I can to sound enthusiastic—for his sake.

Actually—though I hate to admit it—the place looks kind of warm and inviting.

So—for Bob's sake and to be honest—I turn to him and give him my Fenway-Frank opinion.

"Yo!" I tell him. "Yaz!"

He smiles and hugs me close and kisses my forehead.

And just then, Lois's car pops out of the trees and into the clearing.

She pulls up next to us and, climbing out of the car, she explains, "Had to make a pit stop."

"What do you think?" says Bob, nodding over toward the cottage.

"So *far!*" says Esther, unfolding herself from Lois's car.

"No, it's not!" says Bob. "It's just over there. Come on!"

"What about all the stuff?" says Lois.

"Later," says Bob, heading for the cottage.

"Pretty, isn't it?" Lois asks me.

I tell her, "Mm."

And I take off after Bob.

I have a phone call to make.

Forty-one

"Michael?"

"Jess."

The telephone's in the living room.

Which isn't that far from anyplace or *anyone* in the cottage—the cottage being cute but small like it is.

"We just got in," I tell Michael.

"Just now?"

"Yeah," I tell him.

In case there's anybody in the cottage listening, I'm planning to keep my end of the conversation very "Brownies."

Which also happens to be a very good way of not talking to Michael.

Which I still don't want to do.

"It's after five," says Michael.

"Is it?"

"You left before two," he says.

"How do you know?" I ask him.

"I called," he says.

172

"You did?"

"To tell you I missed you," he says.

"That was nice."

"I love you, Jess."

"That's nice, too," I admit.

"You really think so?" he says.

"Mmm," I answer.

"Is that a 'yes'?"

"That's a 'definitely,'" I tell him.

"Just checking," he smiles.

Time to change the subject.

"You know when you're coming up yet?" I ask him.

"Soon as I can," he says.

"Yeah," I answer. "But when will that be?"

"Soon as possible."

"Michael!"

"I'll probably find out around Wednesday. If Sandy doesn't get anything lined up, they want us back at Mr. E's. But I've got to let them know by Thursday."

"That's great," I tell Michael. "About Mr. E's."

"Yeah," Michael grins. "I—"

"Excuse me. I need the line. I'm expecting an important call."

"Huh?"

There's some woman on the phone!

Some woman who's jumped into our conversation.

Without a click!

She's been listening to our conversation.

"I said—" she says.

"You got a party line?" Michael asks me.

"A what?" I answer.

"A party line," this woman says. *"Yes, she does. And I need it free for a very important call."*

I can't believe it!

"Well, ma'am," says Michael, turning on his Southern charm, "if you could give us a couple of seconds alone, I'm sure we could conclude our business."

"Business?" she humphs.

"Of course," Michael tells her, "the longer you're on the line, the longer it will take us to finish up and say our good-byes."

"I'm expecting an important call!" she insists.

"Beg your pardon, ma'am, but this happens to be an important call to us."

"Well!" she gasps. *"We'll just see about that!"*

And with that, she slams down her phone.

There's a second before anybody says anything.

It's as if we were waiting for this woman to jump back on the line.

But when she doesn't—when the second's passed—Michael and I just crack up.

Then, Michael says, "Can't wait to meet your neighbors."

"Me neither," I tell him.

And then, getting serious, Michael asks me for my phone number, and I give it to him.

Then he tells me he'll call me around this time Wednesday. "Just in case Matilda Busybody's expecting another important call," he says.

"We'll be waiting," I tell Michael.

"Wednesday," he says.

"About this time," I say.

"Yeah," he says. "I miss you, Jess."

"Me, too," I tell him.

"'Bye," he says.

"'Bye."

As I hang up the phone, I know—right away—I won't be able to sleep tonight.

I'll be thinking about Michael.

And I'll be waiting for my period.

Not a great combination if you want to get to sleep.

Kind of like a pizza with pepperoni and hot fudge.

But the way it turns out, I'm wrong.

First, there's all the stuff to be lugged in from the cars—stuff to unpack and stick into drawers and closets and cabinets.

174

Then, there's dinner—to make and get through and clean up after.

In fact, by the time I throw my weary bones onto the lumpy little bed I've won in the family lottery, I feel like today has been at least a week long.

Out my window, I can hear the waves, lapping against the shore of the lake.

I start counting them.

Before the third wave hits, I'm out like a light.

Forty–two

"Early to bed, early to rise
Makes a girl ready to scrub the kitchen floor . . ."
                    Mrs. Benjamin Franklin

The thing about summer homes is they're empty three seasons of the year.

So they're really empty houses more than they're summer homes.

The way you turn an empty house into a summer home is, you use a lot of soap and water and polish and elbow grease.

It's like, if you want to get an empty house to look and smell and feel like a summer home, you've got to get it looking and smelling and feeling like a hospital first.

So that's how Lois and Bob and Grandma and I spend the first part of our first glorious day in beautiful White Lake—airing the place out, thumping the rugs, washing the windows, scrubbing the floors and polishing everything that doesn't move.

Not too long after lunch, everything seems to be rounding into shape. We haven't got the bells and the paging system for the doctors installed yet. But the place is really starting to look and smell and feel like "General Cottage."

I decide it's a good time to take a break.

I tell Lois—who doesn't mind—that I'm going to go off, exploring.

Actually, I want to go down to the lake and sit by myself and think things over.

So here I am, sitting out at the end of our little dock with my feet dangling in the water, looking out over this pretty little blue-green lake that's set in this forest of very tall green trees that march right down to the water's edge.

Along the rim of the lake, among the trees, I can see a dotted line of other people's little cottages and houses and docks and boats.

I can also see some of these other people—hanging out in their yards and on their docks and fooling around with their boats.

There are even a few people out in the middle of the lake—fishing, I guess—sitting very still in little boats that bob up and down in the wake of this one speedboat that keeps racing back and forth, towing a kid on water skis.

And then, there's me—Michael's girl, the one who's afraid she won't get her period, the one who's afraid she can't hang on to her man, the one who's dangling her feet in the cold water, hoping it will—somehow—cool her out.

I close my eyes and heave a heavy sigh and tell myself "Relax! It's a pretty day. School's out, and you're in a pretty place. A beautiful place, in fact. Enjoy it. At least, try."

Okay, okay—
I'm in a pretty place.
A beautiful place.
There's cool water all around me.
And warm sunshine on my face.
"Jessie!"
It's Lois.
Calling from the porch.
Beautiful!
"I'm going into town for groceries. You want to come along?"
"Sure!" I shout.
What else have I got to do around here?
But wait for tomorrow?
And Michael's call?
And my period?
"I'd love to," I shout.
But just now—as I clump up the dock and trudge up the path to Lois's car—I've got a feeling it's going to be a very long summer.

Forty-three

By the time Lois and I get into town—it's only about a five-minute ride—but by then, I'm feeling a little better.

The thing is, if you had to pick a place to be away from Michael in, you really couldn't do much better than this.

White Lake—what there is of it—is mostly these very old wooden buildings—little shops and stores and a volunteer fire station and a couple of old hotels with sloping verandas and great wide lawns—all huddled together down at one end of the lake.

Along Main Street—which they could have named *Only* Street or *The* Street, as far as I can see—there are all kinds of people—old people, middle-aged people and kids—not a crowd of people, but enough people to make it look fairly busy.

All these people are dressed real comfortable and casual, and everybody seems relaxed and happy, and—maybe because the whole town's only about three blocks long—nobody seems like they're in a rush to get anywhere.

"Looks nice," I admit.

Lois gives me a grateful smile.

"I think so, too," she says.

"You want to buy a General?" I ask her.

"I don't think so," she says.

"Oh."

"Why?"

"Because we just passed a General Store," I tell her.

"With groceries?"

"Uh-huh."

"Do you want to buy a General?" she asks me.

I consider it for a second and then, coming to a decision, I tell Lois, "I think so."

"Okay," she says.

"And some groceries," I add.

"As long as we're there," she agrees.

"And some Tampax," I say.

"Oh," says Lois, nodding her head.

Like having milk and cookies waiting for Santa Claus, I figure having Tampax around the cottage will make my period feel wanted and welcome.

"I forgot to pack it," I explain.

"I need some, too," Lois admits.

"Experienced travelers!" I laugh.

Lois laughs, too.

"Women of the world!" she says.

Turning around, Lois finds us a parking place right in front of the General Store.

Actually, the General Store is a pretty incredible place to be in—with everything in the world cluttering up the shelves and hanging from the walls and ceilings and standing in the middle of the aisles.

While Lois buys out the grocery department, I wander around, taking it all in, looking for the drug department, where I expect to find the Tampax I'm looking for.

After a while, wandering around—inspecting the inflatable boats and the bolts of flannel and the pitchforks and fishing reels—I bump into the drug department and start looking around for the Tampax section.

And that's when I spot it.

Incredible!

Why didn't I think of it before?

Quick-As-A-Bunny!
The Do-It-Yourself Test for Early Pregnancy

For just a few dollars, I can buy this little magic box and find out, once and for all, whether I've really got anything to worry about.

But how many dollars is just a few?

I pick up the box—it fits right into my hand—and I start looking for a label with the price.

"Find it?"

"Huh?"

Lois!

Coming up behind me!

Quick-as-a-bunny—so she won't see what I've been up to—I suck in my stomach, pull out my belt, stuff the box down inside the top of my jeans, fluff my top up over it and—as I dash down the aisle to the Tampax section and grab a couple of boxes—I hit her with a barrage of chatter.

"Yeah! Right! Tampax! Right over here! Lots of it! Done with your shopping already? Some store, huh? Here!"

She looks at the boxes I'm holding out to her.

"Gauze?" she asks me.

I look at the boxes.

They're gauze, all right.

"I wanted to get something for my *mummy*," I tell Lois.

"Jessie!" she gasps, breaking up in spite of herself. "That's awful!"

"Yeah," I admit. "It *sphinx*, doesn't it?"

That does it.

Lois claps her hand to her chest, rolls her eyes and—in an Irish brogue I've never heard her use before—she cries, "Saints preserve us!"

Which breaks me up.

And gets me off the hook.

Quickly, I move up the aisle and swap the gauze for a couple of boxes of Tampax.

Then—with my *Quick-As-A-Bunny!* test kit stuffed inside the top of my jeans—I move past the cash register, out the door and into A Life of Wickedness and Crime!

Forty–four

I know it's no defense, Your Honor, but I never meant to steal the Quick-As-A-Bunny! Do-It-Yourself Test For Early Pregnancy.

I meant to buy it.

Not right then, but the next time I was in the General Store—the next time I was in there alone.

That's why I was checking for the price.

Until Lois walked up and I had to act fast.

In self-defense, you might say.

It costs twelve ninety-five, Your Honor.

Once I got home and up to my little room and closed the door and pulled the box out from inside my jeans and checked it out again, I found the label with the price.

It was conveniently located at the bottom of the box, Your Honor.

As soon as I saw the price, I made a promise to myself.

I promised myself, one way or another, before the

summer was over, I'd make sure the General Store got its twelve ninety-five back from me.

That's the promise I made myself, Your Honor.

And I'd make the same promise to you.

If you'd let me keep my Quick-As-A-Bunny! Do-It-Yourself Test For Early Pregnancy.

Yes, Your Honor.

You have my solemn oath.

I swear the General Store will get its twelve ninety-five back.

I swear.

Thank you, Your Honor.

You'll never regret it.

Forty–five

It's after dinner.

We ate in White Lake.

At this little place that specializes in Italian food.

Which I ate too much of.

Anyway, now I'm up in my room, all washed up and almost ready for bed.

But the thing is, I'd really like to take this test and find out if I'm pregnant or not.

Especially if I'm not.

But I'm also thinking—if, instead of doing it right now, I wait until the end of the day, tomorrow—maybe I'll get my period by then.

And then, I'll know I'm not pregnant.

And then, the day after tomorrow, I'll find a way to smuggle the unopened *Quick-As-A-Bunny!* box back into the General Store and sneak it back onto the shelf where I found it, without anybody noticing.

But meanwhile, I've got to find a place to stash the box, a place where nobody will find it.

I could hide it outside somewhere, far from the cottage, where nobody would think to look.

But if I did, there's a chance it might get rained on, or ants might get into it, or bears, or something.

I could hide it somewhere around the house, too.

But we haven't lived here long enough for me to have figured out where nobody'd ever think to go poking around.

So, I decide to hide it right here, in my own little room.

It's true that my room's pretty small. But it's also true that it's mine. So nobody's very likely to come nosing around here.

At least, not tonight.

But where in my little room should I hide it?

Of course!

I drop down under my bed and squeeze the box up between the mattress and the springs and wrap the tail of the sheet around it so no one can see it, even if they just happen to be hanging out under my bed.

Then, just to test my hiding place, I crawl out from under the bed and lie down on it.

Perfect!

Quick-As-A-Bunny! isn't anymore.

Now it's nothing more than one lump among the many lumps in my lumpy little bed.

Except—because it's the lump with all the answers—it's my favorite lump.

I pat its little head and wish it good night and close my eyes and sleep.

Forty-six

Here's a riddle for a Wednesday—
 Why is Jessie Walters like a run-on sentence?
 Here's the answer—
 She's missing a period.
 So far, anyway.
 That was the first thing I thought of—and the first thing I checked out—when I woke up this morning.
 But then I told myself—just because you're like a run-on sentence this morning, that doesn't mean you have to be like a run-on sentence tomorrow, or even ten minutes from now.
 Which is true.
 I mean, periods are like substitute teachers.
 Just because they don't show up on time, that doesn't mean they're not going to show up at all.
 I mean, even if you're super regular—which I'm not—but even if you are, there are lots of things that can throw your timing off.

Things like tension—which I've been feeling a lot of lately.

And traveling—which I did quite a lot of, just the day before yesterday.

And lots of other things—like, probably, even drinking different water than the kind you're used to.

And stuff like that.

In fact, I guess almost anything can mess up the timing of your period.

So I tell myself, it's too soon to panic.

Even tomorrow's too soon to panic.

But Friday?

Well, that's a long way off.

Two whole days.

And meanwhile, I've promised Bob I'd let him teach me how to cook on a barbecue tonight.

It's one of Bob's all-time favorite things—teaching me how to cook on a barbecue.

He teaches it to me at the start of every summer.

And then, of course, for the rest of the summer, Bob insists on doing all the barbecuing himself.

Which is fine with me.

Because Bob loves to cook on a barbecue.

And he's great at it.

So at the start of every summer, when Bob offers to teach me how to cook on a barbecue, I just go along for the ride and do whatever I can to help him have a good time for himself.

But this year—because we're not home, where Bob's got his own prized barbecue—there's actually something for me to do.

Unfortunately, what I've got to do is clean up this grungy old barbecue that Bob's found, stored under the back porch.

Even though this barbecue is all caked up with this corroding charcoal from about the Year One and it's got these patches of rust and gunk all over the grill, Bob says if I clean it up, it will work fine and get us through the summer without our having to buy a barbecue we don't really need.

So that's my job and that's what I'm doing when the phone rings inside the cottage.

It's about five o'clock, so I figure it's probably Michael.

A couple of seconds pass.

"Jessie?"

It's Lois, leaning out the back door.

"For you," she says.

And she ducks back inside.

It is Michael!

Calling to tell me when he's coming up.

I've got this muck that I've been hacking out of the bottom of the barbecue all over my hands.

But Michael's waiting.

To tell me he's coming up right after the weekend.

"Jessie! Your hands!"

Lois catches me racing into the kitchen.

I've left my hand prints all over the door.

"Sorry."

"He'll wait," she tells me, walking over to the sink. She picks up a bar of soap and says, "Here."

"I'll use this," I tell Lois. And I grab the dishcloth from the sink and split for the living room.

Michael's waiting!

I hear Lois scolding me from the kitchen—"Jessie!"—as I pick up the phone.

"Hi, Michael."

"Hi, Jess."

There's something wrong!

I can tell!

I can hear it in his voice!

"What's up?" I ask him.

"Oh," he says, making his voice sound a little brighter, "lots of stuff."

"Like what?"

"Well," he says, "for one thing, it's official. We

signed the contract today. The Skye Band's got a manager."

"Sandy?"

"Yup."

"Congratulations."

"Thanks," he says. "But . . ."

Here it comes!

"But what?" I ask him.

"Nothing," he says. "Only, it looks like Sandy's going to be keeping us pretty busy."

"Oh?"

"We're starting out in Yonkers over the weekend."

"That's near here, isn't it?"

"The same general direction," he concedes. "But . . ."

"But what, Michael?"

"We're playing Saturday, Sunday, Monday and Tuesday."

"Uh-huh."

"And then, Thursday—" he says.

"Thursday?"

"Yeah," he says, "we're playing in Pennsylvania. Lancaster. Ever heard of it?"

"No."

"Me neither," he says.

"What about Wednesday?" I ask him.

"Well—we don't finish Tuesday until three or four in the morning. That's Wednesday morning. And then, we've still got to break down and pack up and haul ass about two hundred miles to Lancaster before we crash for the night.

"Then, the next day—Thursday—we've got to get up and find the place we're playing at and set up so we can play again that night."

"On the way from Yonkers to Lancaster, will you be stopping by White Lake?"

"Not this time, Jess."

"I didn't think so."

190

"There'll be other times," ne tells me.

"You sure?" I ask him.

"As sure as I am that I love you," he says.

"How sure is that?" I ask him.

"Hey!" he says. "Lighten up."

"I was just asking," I tell him.

"Jess, I'm doing the best I can. You know?"

"I know," I admit. "I'm sorry. I guess I just . . ."

"Miss me?"

"Yeah."

"Love me?"

"Yeah."

"Think of me all the time?"

"How did you know?" I ask him.

"It's the same with me," he says. "And listen, Sandy can't keep us going like this all the time. You know that. And the second it eases up—"

"Michael?"

"Yeah?"

"What if I needed to talk to you? How would I know where you are?"

"Hey! Jess!" he says. "We're talking now, aren't we?"

"Yeah," I admit. "But . . ."

"You'll always know where I am. Because I'll tell you. We're at Hudax in Yonkers. And then, in Lancaster, the place is called Al's and Judy's. Or Judy's and Al's. I forget. But you don't have to worry. Because I'll be calling you. You'll be there, won't you?"

"I guess," I sigh.

"Don't you know?" he asks.

"I guess not."

"This is just a temporary thing, Jess."

"I know."

"We go on and on, remember?"

"Yeah," I tell him.

"We'll be together soon," he says.

"Okay."

"You believe it?"

"Yeah."

"Do you love me?"

"If you only knew," I tell him.

"Tell me," he says.

"I can't."

"You worried about Matilda Busybody?"

"No," I tell him. "My mother."

"Oh. Well . . ." he says.

I can hear him getting restless.

"You have to go?" I ask him.

"We're rehearsing. Over at Mark's."

"Say 'hi' for me."

"I will. . . . Jess?"

"Yeah?"

"If you can't talk and tell me you love me," he says, "could you just kind of blink your eyes to let me know?"

"Michael!"

"You blinking them?" he asks.

"Can't you tell?" I ask him.

"Yeah," he smiles. "Thanks."

"Are you blinking yours?" I ask him.

"Can't you tell?" he says.

"Yeah, I can."

"I'll call you soon, honey."

"Okay."

"Take care," he says.

"You, too," I tell him.

"Love you."

"Mm."

"'Night, Jess."

"'Night, Michael."

Hanging up the phone, I take a deep breath and I tell myself it's time to face it.

What just happened—Michael breaking our date— that's probably just the beginning.

Sandy Shore's probably going to keep Michael so

busy playing and traveling around all summer—he'll never have time to get away.

Michael will never have time to be with me.

Not until the summer's over.

And then, he'll go off to Michigan, to music school.

So I won't see him when summer's over, either.

I probably won't see him again until Christmas vacation.

Unless he goes to Fort Lauderdale, or somewhere, like lots of college kids do.

He probably will.

I wonder if it would make any difference.

If I really was pregnant.

Instead of just thinking I might be.

I wonder.

If I really was pregnant, wouldn't Michael just drop everything and come to see me?

I wonder.

Should I go on wishing I'm *not* pregnant?

Or should I start wishing I am?

Or doesn't it make any difference?

It doesn't.

If it made any difference, Michael would be here with me—holding me and comforting me—now, when I really need him.

Forty–seven

I've waited all day.

It's Thursday night, and I've waited all day long.

It didn't work.

Not opening my *Quick-As-A-Bunny!* Do-It-Yourself Test For Early Pregnancy didn't get my run-on sentence punctuated.

As a matter of fact, it's beginning to look like what I might be up against here is what they call an Undeterminate Sentence.

Which means it's time for me to stop messing around.

It's time for me to open up my *Quick-As-A-Bunny!* box and read the instructions and take the test.

It's time to find out if I'm just a former virgin or if I'm also a formerly unpregnant person, as well.

It's especially time to find this out, now that I've talked to Michael.

Now that we've talked, I've got to admit—like it or not—it's possible I'll never see the father of my maybe baby ever again.

So it's time.

Time to find out, once and for all.

Am I or am I not pregnant?

Sitting on my lumpy little bed with my back to the door, I tell myself, "Well, here goes nothing—I hope!"

And I open up my *Quick-As-A-Bunny!* box.

Inside it, I find this miniature laboratory and this piece of paper with all the instructions written on it.

I have to admit, as I struggle to unfold the instruction sheet and find the place where the instructions begin, I'm what you'd have to call extremely tense.

In fact, the way my hands are shaking—if I ever get the instruction sheet unfolded and figure out where I'm supposed to start reading—I'm not sure I'll be able to hold it steady enough to read.

The thing is, I'm probably just seconds away from learning the Awful (or Wonderful) Truth.

I mean, finding out if I'm pregnant or not has got to affect the way I'm going to live from now on, for the whole rest of my life.

So you can understand.

Why I'm having such a hard time finding—

There!

That's where the instructions begin.

Here goes.

Nothing.

I hope.

I get my hope.

Here's the first thing the instructions say—

IMPORTANT:
This test is not effective if administered less than

*nine days after the day on which you expected your
last period.*

Terrific, right?

Just what I needed, right?

Perfect.

Quick-As-A-Bunny!

Ha!

By the time this thing tells me if I'm pregnant, my
baby may be wondering if *she's* pregnant.

But on the other hand, there isn't much I can do
about it, is there?

So I fold up the instructions and put them back in the
box.

I crawl under the bed and plant the box under the
end of a sheet in Lumpland.

I turn out the light and I promise myself I'll take the
test the minute I wake up—one week from tomorrow.

Quick-As-A-Bunny!

Ha!

Forty-eight

Time passes slowly up here in the mountains . . .

That's a song by Bob Dylan, and one of Michael's favorites.

Bob Dylan used to live up here in the Catskill Mountains.

And believe me, he knows what he's talking about.

In the time it takes to get from yesterday to next Friday—when I plan to take the *Quick-As-A-Bunny!-* Ha! test—you could probably raise yourself a nice crop of century plants—from seed.

For instance, right now, it's about eight o'clock Saturday night.

Around seven—which seems like a year or two ago—Bob drove Lois and Grandma into Monticello.

In Monticello—which Bob says is French for a mountain that's shaped like a cello, and which is about fifteen miles from here—Bob and Lois and Grandma are going to see a movie I've already seen and didn't like that much the first time.

So I'm sitting here, watching television and sending Michael these "Call Jessie now!" messages by ESP and eating a peanut-butter-and-banana sandwich.

It's actually my third peanut-butter-and-banana sandwich tonight.

My third since dinner.

I've been eating a lot lately.

I'm worried about it.

About where I get the appetite from.

And worrying about it just seems to make me hungrier.

It's a vicious circle.

Like my waistline.

Anyway—

The phone rings.

And it *is* Michael!

Incredible!

He's at Hudax, in Yonkers, and he's just about to do his first show since Sandy Shore became his manager and he's thinking of it as something like his "professional debut."

So Michael's a little nervous.

And he admits it.

To me.

Which is sweet.

And he tells me how much he really misses me.

Which is also sweet.

And he asks me to wish him luck and to close my eyes and wish him a kiss.

Which is the sweetest of all.

But it's more than Matilda Busybody can take.

Right!

She's been listening in all along.

And we had no idea.

But now—when she barks, *"Disgusting!"* and slams her phone down—we both just break up!

"I'm gonna have to start writing you letters." Michael laughs. "I mean, if I said half the things I'm thinking about you right now—about you and a big dark room with maybe a fireplace and soft music and a great big bed—"

"Michael!"

"Matilda would probably foam at the mouth," he laughs, "and run around in circles, and fall down on the floor—dead but smiling at last."

"At least that'd keep her off the line," I laugh.

"I've got to start writing letters," he says, like it's his New Year's resolution.

"You've got to start coming to *see* me, too," I remind him.

"Oh, Jess," he says, his voice suddenly sad and filled with longing. "I wish I was with you right now."

"Me, too," I tell him.

"I wish you were in my arms right now."

"I'll always love you, Michael."

"Good night, honey."

"Be wonderful tonight, Michael."

"I love you, Jess."

Forty–nine

When I was using ESP, trying to get Michael to call me, I figured talking to him was just what I needed.

I thought if we could talk, it might pull me out of the funk I've been in.

But it didn't work out like I thought.

Because all the while I was talking to Michael—hearing his voice, imagining his face, his eyes, his mouth—I could feel this awful longing stirring down deep inside me.

And even now, now that we've finished talking—this awful longing hasn't stopped.

And it's so deep and needful.

So hungering.

It's like an ache.

An ache that finally drives me to my bed.

To what peace I can find.

Before—

At last—

I dream myself to sleep.

Fifty

Time passes slowly up here in the mountains . . .

Not that I'm at a loss for things to fill my time with.
  I've got Michael to fill my time with.
  Thinking about Michael.
  Daydreaming about Michael.
  Finding ways to remind myself of Michael.

Time passes slowly up—Ugh!

For example, I'm trying to teach myself how to play
"Time Passes Slowly" on the guitar Michael gave me
for my birthday.
  It would be nice if I could surprise Michael and play
it for him the next time I see him.
  If I don't have arthritis by then.
  It isn't all that easy, figuring out what the chords
are or where they come in the song.
  But the way time's passing—slowly—what do I care?
  And the other thing is, trying to learn one of

Michael's favorite songs on the guitar he gave me—his guitar—reminds me of Michael.

The guitar, especially.

It's been part of Michael.

So at least, when I'm holding Michael's guitar, part of me is touching part of him.

And since there's not much chance of its going any farther—between our two parts, I mean—it's really sweet.

Our parts touching.

It reminds me how much I truly love Michael.

And how I couldn't bear it if I lost him.

Time passes slowly up—Ugh!

Maybe it will come to me later.

The chord I can't figure out.

But for now, I put the guitar aside.

"'Bye, Michael."

And life goes on.

Slowly.

One day, I go out with Grandma to look for a spot where she can start her vegetable garden.

Just up the road that leads from the cottage to the highway, through this break in the trees that line the road, Grandma and I find this big open field with nothing in it but tall grass and—off to one side—a bunch of gnarled old apple trees.

There's this kind of track that runs through the field—this memory of a road made by the wheels of horse-drawn farm machinery back in the day when the field was part of a working farm.

Grandma and I follow this track over to a spot near the apple trees.

I've carried this shovel with me all the way from the cottage, so—when we got to wherever Grandma thought her garden should be—I could dig up the grass and Grandma could take a good look at the soil underneath it.

So that's what I do now.

I dig the shovel into the ground underneath the tall grass and—stomping down on the blade with my foot—I turn over this big clump of dirt and roots and tall grass.

And there—where the clump used to be—is the soil for Grandma's garden—looking reddish-brown, raw and rich.

Getting to her knees, Grandma lifts a handful of the soil in her fingers, closes her eyes, smells it and smiles. She offers it to me.

I smell it. I'm surprised. It's dirt but it smells sweet and nice and clean.

So it's decided.

This will be the spot for Grandma's garden.

The only problem now is how we get a plow into the field to turn over the soil.

"Come," says Grandma. "Let's see where it leads."

She's talking about this same track that runs through the field.

So we set out to see where it takes us and—as we're walking—I remember this story Grandma told me once, this true-life story that happened to her when she was a girl about my age, back in Russia.

Grandma told me the story as a way of telling me she knew what I was going through—the changes I was going through with Michael, and being in love with him and everything.

She wanted me to know that I wasn't the only person in the world who'd ever gone through what I was going through.

And she also wanted me to know that what I was going through was just as important as anything anybody ever went through.

The boy in Grandma's story—the older boy that Grandma was in love with when she was my age, back in Russia—was named *Duvid*—which is Russian or Jewish, or both, for David.

So—because that story reminds me of Michael and all we've been through and all we're going through now—I say, "What was his name again, Grandma?"

And she says, "Whose name?"

"Duvid," I say, like I just remembered it.

"Duvid?" she laughs. "You remember?"

"Grandma!" I tell her. "It's one of my favorite stories. In fact—would you mind telling it to me again?"

She stops where we're walking along this track, in the middle of this big open field.

Smiling at me—like she loves me and she's proud of me—she raises her hand and touches my cheek.

But now, still smiling, she shakes her head and says, "No. Today is for tomorrow, not for yesterday.

"Look!" she says.

And I look where she's pointing.

Just a little way up the track, I can see the highway.

Grandma's plow could ride right up the highway and follow the old wagon track straight to the spot near the apple trees where Grandma wants her garden.

"All right!" I shout, and I give Grandma a hug to congratulate her on finding a way for a plow to get into the field and because—even if she didn't tell me the story I wanted to hear—she did remind me of Michael.

"Today is for tomorrow, not for yesterday."

Maybe I shouldn't be thinking so much about what happened between Michael and me before—yesterday.

Maybe I should start thinking about how to make what happens next, happen better—tomorrow.

Time passes slowly up here in the mountains.
We sit beside bridges and walk beside foun-
*   tains—Ugh!*

204

One morning before the sun comes up, I haul myself out of bed to go fishing with Bob.

I don't fish.

I just go along for the ride.

Bob fishes.

He sits with me out in the middle of the lake, dangling a painted metal lure over the side of the boat.

He does this from the time the sun rises until it's risen straight up over our heads.

And then we go back to the cottage.

Bob's caught nothing.

Not one fish.

Which isn't that surprising.

"Fisherman" Bob's never gone fishing before.

This was his first time.

But the thing is, our summer cottage came equipped with a little rowboat and an aluminum-foil motor and a couple of fishing reels that we found stashed in the kitchen closet.

And here Bob was, vacationing next to this fish-filled lake.

So—

Since he had all the equipment—

And since he had the occasion—

Bob felt like he just had to give it a try.

It reminds me of someone I know.

Of her last night with Michael.

And how maybe she's just a chip off the old block, after all.

Time passes slowly up here in the mountains.
We sit beside bridges and walk beside fountains.
We catch the wild fishes that—Ugh!

I'm helping Lois with *her* garden this morning.

It's a flower garden.

It's not a big rectangle like Grandma's garden's going to be.

205

It's just this narrow strip of ground that runs all around the cottage.

Lois has already taken some flowering plants she bought at a plant nursery and plugged them into strategic spots along the narrow strip of ground.

But now she wants to put in some seeds that will grow into flowers and fill out the spaces between her widely spaced store-boughts.

So we're down on our hands and knees—Lois and me—making these little trenches in the soil and popping in these tiny seeds and tucking them in with the dirt left over from the trenches we've made.

I don't know why—maybe it's the seeds and the way they remind me of my maybe baby—but I start crying.

And the next thing I know, Lois is kneeling next to me and asking me what's wrong.

I tell her, "I guess I miss Michael."

Which—as far as it goes—is the truth.

"Ooh," she says, feeling for me, making my pain her own.

And, taking me in her arms, she hugs me and asks, "Where is he now?"

"He's supposed to be in Lancaster," I tell her.

"Supposed to be?"

"I haven't talked to him since last Saturday," I tell her.

"He was nervous about going out to play his first performance since Sandy Shore became his manager."

"Well," she says, leaning back away from me, "that makes sense."

"He opens in Lancaster tonight."

"Pennsylvania?"

"Yeah."

"So," she says, "he might be calling you."

"Yeah," I say, "he might. I just miss him, that's all."

"Well," she says, touching my cheek, just like Grandma, "you might miss him less if you got out a little and gave yourself a chance to make a few friends. In time, you might even get to like it here."

"How much time?" I ask her.

"Too much?" she guesses.

I nod my head and laugh a hopeless little grunt of a laugh.

Lois sighs and, smiling sadly, she says, "Well, if we get back to work, maybe—when you see Michael again—you can bring him a bouquet of fresh flowers."

It's a sweet thought.

And Lois has been very sweet to me.

I hug her one last time.

For trying to cheer me up.

And because I don't want her to see me fighting back tears.

Time passes slowly up here in the mountains.
We sit beside bridges and walk beside fountains.
We catch the wild fishes that float through the stream.
Time passes slowly when you're lost in a dream . . .

Fifty-one

Michael didn't call last night.

I didn't expect him to.

I was just hoping he would, that's all.

Because he missed me.

And wanted to hear my voice.

And because I was scared.

About the test.

Quick-As-A-Bunny!

Today's the day.

Last night—after Michael didn't call—I got out the instructions for the test and read myself to sleep over them.

It's a good thing I did.

Because the first thing I had to do this morning was—excuse me, Matilda—but the first thing I had to do was collect three drops of my urine.

Actually, more, but you need three for the test.

So I got up early—like I was going out fishing with "Fisherman" Bob.

The test only takes two hours, and I figured I could take it and get it done before everybody woke up so nobody'd have to know what I was up to—collecting my urine, and everything.

So here I am, standing with my back to the door— which I've closed and locked with this old hook-and-eye lock it's got attached to it—standing at the dresser in front of my window.

What I'm doing is concentrating.

It takes a lot of concentration.

This *Quick-As-A-Bunny!* Do-It-Yourself Test For Early Pregnancy.

Because you've got to do everything—every step of the test—just right.

If you goof up, even if it's just a little, you have to throw the test out and get another one and start all over again.

So I'm concentrating on this miniature laboratory that was packed inside the *Quick-As-A-Bunny!* box— this laboratory that was designed to be used by scientists under two feet tall.

Everything in it—the test tube, the test-tube stopper, the stand to hold the test tube, the eyedropper, the packet of chemicals—it all comes straight from Teenytown.

And here I am—this giant-sized nonscientist—and all I've got to do is juggle all these Teenytown toys the first time out without a slip!

I close my eyes.

I say a silent, wordless prayer.

And the test begins.

The first thing I have to do is the trickiest thing.

I guess that's so you can blow it at the top and get it over with.

What I've got to do is this—

Using this eensy eyedropper they gave me, I've got to drop three—not three and a half, not two and three-quarters—but *exactly three drops* of urine into this teensy test tube I've got set up in this teensy test-tube stand.

And—

Now, get *this,* Nervous First-Time User!—

I've got to drop these exactly three drops of urine into the teensy test tube, without any part of the eensy eyedropper touching any part of the teensy test tube.

Or I blow it.

The whole test.

Neat, huh?

It's like throwing darts at a house fly!

Impossible!

But necessary.

So—

I close one eye, poise the eensy eyedropper over the teensy test tube, take a deep breath, let it out slow, stop my breathing, open the eye I closed, readjust my aim and squeeze (One!) squeeze (Two!) squeeze (Three, Exactly!) drops—*Bam! Bam! Bam!*—right into the teensy test tube, without the eensy eyedropper ever coming anywhere near it.

Whew!

Okay.

Now what?

Keep the test tube on a flat surface, away from vibrations and sunlight.

Sunlight!

Here I am, with everything set up on the dresser in front of the window, through which—the second it comes up—the sun will start flooding in!

I've got to move!

Quick!

Careful!

Where?

My closet!

On the floor.

In the back.

Whew!

That was close.

Thank goodness the sun wasn't up yet.

If it was up, and I'd poured the tiny packet of chemicals into the teensy test tube, that would have done it!

I would have blown it right there.

So—

Okay.

I'm lying on the floor in the back of my closet with just a little bit of lamplight filtering through the open door—just enough to see what I'm doing—and I pour the chemicals into the test tube.

Now—

Insert the test-tube stopper and shake well for at least ten seconds.

At least ten seconds.

Right.

One thousand one—

Please!

One thousand two—

Just this once!

One thousand three—

I'm sorry!

One thousand four—

I shouldn't have!

One thousand five—

But I couldn't help it!

One thousand six—

Michael's so wonderful!

One thousand seven—

I thought I'd lose him!

One thousand eight—

Oh, please!

One thousand nine—

Don't let me lose him!
One thousand ten—
Don't let me be pregnant!
One thousand—
Please?
Eleven!
One for good measure.
Okay.
Now—
The teensy test tube goes back into the teensy test-tube stand.
And it sits there.
Undisturbed.
Without vibrations.
Or sunlight.
For two hours.
It sits there with all the chemicals percolating.
If I'm not pregnant, after two hours, this dark reddish-brown stuff will fall in a heap at the bottom of the test tube.
If I am pregnant, after two hours, this reddish-brown stuff will fall in a ring, like a little reddish-brown bicycle tire, at the bottom of the test tube.
Which gives me two hours to—
What?
What do you do while you're waiting to find out if you're pregnant or not?
Play "Time Passes Slowly" on Michael's guitar?
That wouldn't help.
And it would wake everybody up.
And it would remind me of Michael.
It might be bad luck to be thinking about Michael while these chemicals are percolating.
I don't want to give them any ideas.
So what can I do that won't remind me of Michael?
Sneak downstairs to the kitchen and make up a big surprise breakfast for everybody?
Go for a sunrise swim?

The sun is up now.

Not in here.

Not on the floor in the back of my dark closet, where the answer to the most important question in my life is percolating in this teensy test tube.

In here, it's dark and warm and cedary.

Mmm.

Maybe, what I should do is just stretch out here and wait for the answer to reveal itself.

Yeah . . .

Maybe . . . Muh . . . Ummmmmmmmzzzzzzzzzzzz zzzzzzzzzzzz . . .

Voices.

Far off and familiar.

Like voices in a dream . . .

"I don't know. I haven't seen her."

"Maybe she got up early and went out."

"Jessie?"

"She might."

"How much you want to bet she's still upstairs asleep?"

"A zucchini."

"I've got an idea . . ."

Thump! Thump!

Bob!

Coming up the stairs.

The test!

Wait.

I close my eyes.

Please! Please! Please!

I . . .

Open . . .

My eyes . . .

No ring!

No little reddish-brown bicycle tire!

I'm all right!

Thank you! Thank you! Thank you!

All right!

Bob—!

"Bob!" I shout from the floor at the back of my closet.

"Jess?" he says.

He's standing in the hallway outside my door. He's heard the excitement in my voice, and I guess he's puzzled by it.

But—now that I think of it—I'm puzzled, too.

It's not over.

I'm not okay.

Unless—

"You okay?" he says.

"It depends," I tell him. "What time is it?"

"Uh," he says—checking his watch while I hold my breath. "Would you be okay if it was a quarter after ten?"

"Yeah."

"You're okay," he says.

"Thanks," I tell him, breathing again.

"Don't mention it," he says.

"I won't," I promise.

"Thanks," he says.

"Don't mention it," I tell him.

"Don't mention what?" he says.

"Sorry, I promised not to mention it."

"Oh. Well, then," he says, "I guess I'll go finish my breakfast. Will you join us in a cup of coffee?"

It's one of Bob's favorite corny jokes.

"Do you think we'll all fit?" I ask him.

"To get to the other side," he answers.

And I hear him laughing to himself as he turns and walks away, heading for the kitchen and the breakfast he's left waiting.

"I love you, Bob," I call to him.

"I love you, too, kiddo," he shouts.

"Me, too," Lois shouts.

Grandma says something I can't hear.

"Esther loves you, too," Lois shouts, "but she hates shouting."

Which makes me laugh.

Hey!

I'm laughing!

All right!

Okay!

Quick! Stash the test.

Thank you, my lovely little laboratory, my sweet teensy test tube, my adorable eensy eyedropper, my super little instruction sheeeet—

ACCURACY
When Quick-As-A-Bunny! test indicates "Positive-Pregnant":
 Accuracy of test confirmed in 97% of cases surveyed.
When Quick-As-A-Bunny! test indicates "Negative-Not Pregnant":
 Accuracy confirmed in 80% of cases surveyed.
IMPORTANT
If menstruation fails to occur within seven days after "Negative-Not Pregnant" indication, you should purchase another Quick-As-A-Bunny! Do-It-Yourself Test For Early Pregnancy and conduct a follow-up test or consult your personal physician.

Sure.

I'll buy another *Quick-As-A-Bunny!*

Right away.

Hey, just because it's wrong one out of five times, that's no reason to complain.

I might be one of the lucky four.

You never know.

Even if you pay to find out—even if you risk apprehension and imprisonment to find out—you never know.

Isn't that great?

I mean, just think, for only a few dollars, you, too, can find out what I've found out—you never know.

And you can find out you never know, *fast.*

Through a little modern miracle we're proud to call *Quick-As-A-Pickpocket!*

Wonderful!

Great!

Terrific!

Nuts!

Fifty-two

After breakfast, Grandma and I walk out to the big open field we found.

The man with the plow who's going to turn over the soil for Grandma's garden is supposed to meet us out by the gnarled old apple trees.

As we walk out to the field together, I can tell Grandma's all excited about getting her garden started. So I do the best I can to act like I'm excited, too.

But when you're officially an eighty-percent-probably-not-pregnant fourteen-year-old girl, acting like you're excited about your grandmother's garden isn't all that easy.

The best I can do is the best I can do.

But it turns out to be good enough to get Grandma and me out to the field and into the shade of the gnarled old apple trees and up to the moment when Grandma hears something I haven't heard.

"Look," she says, pointing out toward the highway, "here comes our plow!"

Smiling, she takes my arm and walks me out from under the trees to greet the man with the plow.

As he sees us, the man with the plow waves to us and calls, "*Shalom!*"

And—the way it turns out—the man with the plow is actually a boy with a plow.

A boy around Michael's age.

Wearing short khaki shorts and an open shirt and—on top of his long, wavy black hair—this little khaki hat.

"*Shalom!*" Grandma answers him, shouting over the roar of his tractor. "You're an Israeli!"

Smiling down from the seat of the tractor, looking tall and strong and darkly handsome, he shakes his head and corrects Grandma.

He's not just an Israeli.

He's a native-born Israeli!

"*Sabra!*" he says.

Then—spotting me for the first time—he smiles at Grandma and tells her, "If they told me you had such a beautiful daughter, I would have been here sooner. What's her name?"

"Jessie," I call to him. "I'm her granddaughter, and we want the garden over here."

As I wheel around and start walking over to the spot that Grandma's picked, I hear him tell Grandma, "But since I didn't get here so soon, maybe I'll have to stay a little longer."

Then—hearing him throw his tractor into gear—I turn around and see him smiling at me and driving the tractor across the field, following after me.

When we get to the spot Grandma's picked out, Grandma shows Avi—that's his name—what she'd like plowed.

It's a rectangle about a hundred feet long and about fifty feet wide.

"How long do you think it will take you?" I ask him.

He smiles at me and—with his big black eyes—he begins unbuttoning my blouse.

"How long would you like it to take?" he asks.

"As quickly as possible," I tell him.

Still smiling, he drops his eyes to my waist.

"What's the hurry?" he says.

"We're hungry!" I tell him, and—slapping his face with my eyes—I turn to Grandma and tell her, "I'll be back at the cottage."

By the time I get halfway across the clearing, I can hear Avi revving up the tractor—either starting to plow or getting ready to plow or just showing off.

I don't turn back to look because I don't want him to see me and get the wrong idea.

I'm not interested.

Except in Michael.

If you're not Michael, don't bother.

Please.

Thank you.

Actually, the way it works out, Avi's done me a big favor.

He's got me back to the cottage a lot earlier than I planned.

And—when I get back to the cottage—it's there!

Waiting for me.

A letter from Michael.

Actually, it's not a letter.

It's in an envelope—postmarked Yonkers—but it's not a letter.

It's a picture postcard.

On one side, there's a picture of Getty Square, in Yonkers.

On the other side—in this tiny printing, written all over the blank space—it says—

Dear Jess,
I'm sorry, honey. Sorry I couldn't get up to see

you. I miss you all the time and I know you feel the same. I guess even when it's right, like it is with us, love is never easy. It never runs smooth.

But anyway, Jess, it's nice talking to you like this, without Waltzing Matilda horning in every five seconds.

I've got to admit it, though. It's also nice talking to you without hearing the sadness in your voice, talking back to me—reminding me how much I love you, how much I miss you, how much I need you.

I really do need you, Jess.

But just knowing that you're there for me and that you'll always be there for me, like I'll always be there for you—that's got a smile spreading all over my face.

But here's Mark, banging at the door. Time to get back to work, I guess.

The next stop's Judie and Al's, in Lancaster.

I'll talk to you then, and I'll—

> *Always love you,*
> *Michael*

P.S.
First night at Hudax went great.
P.P.S.
Especially the newer stuff.
P.P.P.S.
Wait 'til you hear it!

I thought Michael's letter might make me cry.
Which is why I took it up to my room to read.
But actually, it's a laugh.
"Wait 'til you hear the newer stuff!"
Sure!
Don't have much choice, do I?
I'll have to wait 'til I hear it.
Wait, maybe, forever!
I wonder what it will sound like then?

Fifty-three

Call me Piggy.

It fits.

Which is more than I can say for my jeans.

It's not that they're shrinking, either.

It's that I'm expanding.

Which isn't surprising.

The way I've been eating lately.

It's probably because I'm nervous.

About being twenty-percent-possibly pregnant.

I'm also nervous about my weight, of course.

I mean, at the rate I'm going, by the time it gets to be November, I'll be able to tie a rope around my ankle, fill myself with helium and star in Macy's Thanksgiving Day Parade.

That's how bad it is.

I'm planning to see my "personal physician."

Not about my weight, though.

And not about my nervousness.

I'm planning to see my "personal physician" about being twenty-percent-possibly pregnant.

Where I found him was in the Yellow Pages.

My "personal physician."

His name is J. B. Cooney.

He has offices in White Lake and Swan Lake.

When I choose my "personal physicians," I always lean toward two-lake men.

With two-lake men you get—I don't know—it's a certain feeling of confidence, I guess.

I know *I* do.

Anyway—

I called J. B. Cooney this morning and made an appointment to see him.

Tomorrow morning.

At ten-thirty.

The way I see it—

If you've got *Quick-As-A-Pickpocket!* on one side, telling you you're "Negative-Not-Pregnant"—

But you've got your mirror on the other side, telling you you're starting to look like Dolly Parton, coming, and Maxine Truck, going—

You'd better get yourself—as fast as you can—to the nearest two-lake man you can find.

So—

First thing tomorrow morning, I'll hit the road and stick out my thumb, and it's J. B. Cooney, here I come.

Fifty–four

"No, thanks," I tell Lois.

It's early the next morning, and Lois is offering to make me some breakfast.

"I'm dieting," I explain.

"Oh, good," she smiles. "But you shouldn't starve yourself."

"I know," I tell her. "But I've got to start cutting down. And I've got to start exercising, too."

"Now that you mention it," she says, frowning down at her invisible stomach and giving it a pat.

"You're kidding!" I tell her.

"Well . . ." she says, like she's not so sure.

"Any time you want to swap," I tell her.

She smiles at me.

"Anyway," I say, "I thought I'd start by hiking into White Lake this morning."

"You're actually leaving here?" she says—like she can't believe it.

"Well," I tell her, "I figure, now that there's enough of me to share with the rest of the world—"

She laughs and reminds me, "It's three or four miles each way."

"Yeah," I tell her, shrugging it off like it's nothing.

"What are you going to do when you get there?"

"Oh," I tell her, "probably just have a hot-fudge sundae and walk back home."

"Have a good time," she laughs. "And be sure to walk on the side of the road—"

"—facing the oncoming traffic," I say—completing her advice with the words she's said to me a million times before.

"ESP!" she gasps, pretending she's astounded by the way I've read her mind.

"'B-Y-E!" I answer, spelling it out and waggling my fingers at her.

I turn and head for the front door.

As I hit the porch, she calls, "Be careful!"

"Right!" I shout back to her.

"Right!" I think. "If I'd thought of that before, I wouldn't be here now."

Where I am, now, is walking up the road that leads from the cottage to the highway.

When I get to the highway, I start walking along it—facing the oncoming traffic, of course—until I get around the first bend in the road.

Then I stop and stick out my thumb.

About two minutes later, this Japanese car stops, and this American woman gives me a ride into White Lake.

Ten minutes later, this gray-haired nurse in a white uniform and cap looks up at me from her desk inside this old wooden house on—where else but—Main Street.

"Miss Weller?" she guesses, greeting me with a friendly smile.

It's the name I gave her when I called to make the appointment.

"Yes," I tell her, "Jessie."

I kept the Jessie so I wouldn't look confused and blow the whole thing when somebody called me Gwendolyn.

"Have you visited with us before, Miss Weller?"

"No," I apologize.

"You'll have to fill this out," she smiles, forgiving me and handing me a questionnaire on a clipboard at the same time.

"Sure," I tell her.

I take the clipboard from her, find myself a comfortable chair and start filling out the little mimeographed questionnaire.

Miss

Weller, Jessie (none)

New York City

18+

5′3″

100+

Auburn

Blue

No

No

No

No

No

No

No

No

No

I sign Miss Weller's signature at the bottom of the questionnaire and hand it back to the gray-haired nurse.

"Have a seat," she smiles. "Doctor will be with you in a minute."

"Thank you."

I find a chair near a stack of magazines. I pick one out and start thumbing through it.

After a couple of seconds, the door behind the nurse's desk opens, and a woman and a girl about my age come out.

The girl has her arm in a sling, and there's a cast on her hand.

"Well," says the gray-haired nurse to the girl with the broken hand, "how are we doing?"

"Next week," the girl moans.

"Same time?" the nurse asks the girl's mother.

"Fine," says the mother.

"See you then," says the nurse, jotting the appointment in her calendar.

As the girl and her mother turn and walk out of the office, the gray-haired nurse clips my questionnaire to a folder and carries it into the doctor's office.

After a few seconds, she comes back out and says, "Doctor will see you now."

I say, "Thank you," and—praying my knees won't wobble under me—I stand up and wobble over to the door and into the doctor's office.

The door closes behind me.

"Hello," she says.

J. B. Cooney is a woman!

A two-lake woman!

I never thought—!

"Hi," I say.

J. B. Cooney motions me to a chair opposite her desk.

"What seems to be the problem?" she asks.

I take the chair opposite her and tell her, "Nothing."

"Oh?" she says.

I figured when I got here, I'd ask the doctor to give me a general checkup.

Then, while that was going on, I thought I'd ask the doctor—as a matter of idle curiosity—how you could tell the difference between a body like mine and the body of, say, a pregnant person.

Real casual.

That's what I figured.

"I think I'm pregnant!"

I blurt it out.

Just like that.

And—before the words are out of my mouth—I start sobbing.

Just like I promised myself I wouldn't.

I'm glad it's a woman.

I'm glad J. B. Cooney's a woman.

If she was a man, I'd be mortified.

But if she was a man and I was mortified, I probably wouldn't have broken down like this.

I probably would have just gone right ahead with my general checkup game.

But it's better this way.

With a woman.

Not playing games.

Just blurting it out.

And sobbing.

"It's nothing to worry about," she says, taking my hand.

She's come out from behind her desk and she's sitting in a chair she's pulled up right beside me.

"Medically," she assures me, her voice calm and soothing, "there's nothing to worry about. Either way."

"But it's so—!" I begin.

But I finish with a sob.

"It's okay," she says. "You don't have to frighten yourself with what you imagine anymore. In here, we have no imagining. We have only scientific facts and logical procedures and sensible human beings like you and me. Okay?"

Pulling myself together as best I can, I tell her, "Okay."

"Good," she smiles.

"Now," she says, "when did you expect your period?"

"About two weeks ago," I tell her.

"Mm-hm," she says. "I'll need a specimen of your urine."

"For a test?" I ask her.

"Yes," she says.

"*Quick-As-A-Bunny!?*"

"No," she laughs. "You tried *Quick-As-A-Bunny!?*"

"Yes," I admit.

"And?"

"Negative-Not Pregnant," I tell her.

"Well," she says, "at least that's better than Positive, isn't it?"

"Yes."

"But not good enough," she says. "I agree with you. The bathroom's over there. Take off your clothes and put on a gown. You'll see them stacked on the shelf. Bring me a specimen, and then, I'll examine you and we'll see what's what. Okay?"

I give her all the smile I've got and I say, "Thank you."

"Good," she smiles.

And she stands and offers me her hand.

And I take it and stand and walk over to the bathroom.

Inside the bathroom, I get out of my clothes and hang them on the hook. And pick them up off the floor when they fall. And hang them on the hook again.

I put on one of these short hospital gowns, collect a specimen of my urine and carry it out to J. B. Cooney.

She takes it and puts it aside and tells me to jump up on her examining table.

And the examination begins.

It's an internal examination.

And it's extremely embarrassing and pretty uncomfortable.

228

Kind of a cross between riding a horse and going with a rubber robot.

But right away, J. B. Cooney tells me she doesn't think so.

She doesn't think I'm pregnant.

"Of course," she reminds me, "I can't be absolutely sure until the test comes back. But for what it's worth, *Quick-As-A-Bunny!* and I agree on this one. Negative-Not Pregnant. Get dressed."

I go into the bathroom and get my clothes on and come back out.

"If you call me tomorrow about this time, we'll know for sure," she says, motioning me to the chair across from her.

"But I wouldn't worry too much if I were you," she says. "Not about this time . . . But what about next time?"

"I don't know," I tell her.

"You don't know how to protect yourself against getting pregnant?" she asks.

"No. I do. I mean. I just don't know if there will *be* a next time."

"Oh," she smiles. "There will be. Maybe not this young man. Maybe not this year, even, but—believe me—there's bound to be a next time, and a time after that, and so on. It's too good to give up."

"I guess," I tell her.

"So," she says, "what about next time? What are we going to do to avoid unnecessary nightmares like this one?"

"Keep our legs crossed?" I ask her.

"I don't think so," she laughs.

And then she tells me about The Pill and its sometimes unfortunate side-effects.

And the intrauterine device, which is sometimes painful.

And diaphragms, which are—for many women— clumsy and unsatisfying.

229

And condoms, which are—for many men—clumsy and unsatisfying.

And rhythm, which—because it's so chancy—is sometimes called "Roman Roulette."

And abstinence, which is an okay place to visit when you're young, but you wouldn't want to live there.

I pick condoms.

If it comes up again—

When it comes up again--

However long from now that might be—

I'll *insist* on condoms.

"You won't be too embarrassed to talk about it?" J. B. Cooney asks me.

"It's not talking about it that's embarrassing," I tell her. "I know that now."

"Good," she smiles. "Call me tomorrow morning."

I promise her I won't forget.

To call her.

Or how nice she's been.

"I think you're nice, too," she says. "And you've got a good head on your shoulders. Just remember to use it and you'll be fine. You'll see."

I thank her again and offer to pay her.

Smiling, she takes my arm and leads me out of her office and over to the gray-haired nurse who sits outside her door.

"Five dollars," she tells the nurse.

"It's twenty in New Jersey," I tell her.

"Miss Weller," she says, "this is not New Jersey and—in case you've forgotten—you live in New York City."

Before I can tell her how I just moved to New Jersey, but my residence is still New York City, until I can get my house in New Jersey painted and furnished and fixed up and everything—she smiles and gives me a wink and turns around and disappears back inside her office.

Two-lake women!

230

They're the best!
I knew it all along!

I pay the nurse and head out the door.

I hit the street and set out in search of the perfect hot-fudge sundae.

I'm feeling pretty good.

For the first time in a long time.

In fact—I wouldn't say it out loud, just yet—but I'm thinking, "Maybe my luck is starting to change. . . ."

"Maybe it's going to be all right. . . ."

"Maybe . . ."

"Just maybe."

Fifty-five

I'm not pregnant!
  It's official.
  I called J. B. Cooney.
  Just a second ago.
  And she told me.
  The test came out "Negative."
  Positively!
  Eeeeeeehaw!
  I just found out!
  Just this second!
  It's—what?—about eleven o'clock? It's the first time
all morning I've had the house to myself, or I would
have called her hours ago.
  But I just did.
  And she told me.
  I'm not pregnant.
  Thank you!
  Thank you!
  Thank you, God!

Thank you!
Oh!
I feel so good.
Like I just lost about two hundred pounds.
Eeeeeeehaw!
A party!
That's what this calls for.
An Unbirthday Party!
What have I got to throw myself a party with?
Check the refrigerator.
Hmm.
Ballantine's Ale.
Well, it ain't champagne but it'll do.
I pop the top.
I tilt my head back and take a gulp.
I burp.
Long and loud.
Now I rear back and shout—
"Eeeeeeeeeeeeeehaw!"

Fifty-six

Lancaster, Wilkes-Barre, Buffalo, Oswego, Rome, Waterbury, Norwalk, New Haven, Smithtown, Massapequa—I've seen them all!

As a matter of fact, I can see them all right now.

On the picture postcards Michael's sent me from all these places he's played at.

I've got them spread out on my bed.

I'm trying to figure out which one to reread before I go to sleep.

Not that I have to actually read any of them.

By now, I've got all of them practically memorized.

No. What I really like to do is imagine how it was—how Michael was and what he looked like, how he acted and how he felt—from the time he picked out each of these picture postcards until the time he sent them to live with me.

Holding any postcard in my hand I can see how it was, and hear how it was, and feel it, too.

I can see Michael looking through the rack of postcards in the small-town drugstore or the dimestore or the all-night diner or the smoky poolroom or the bus station newsstand where he bought it.

I can be with Michael, sitting at a desk or a table, or sprawled across his bed, writing to me from his room in the run-down hotel or the neon motel or the cheesy tourist cottage where Sandy's got him and the band staying.

I can see him writing to me, backstage in the dressing room at the place he's playing or after hours in the bar, or sitting out front at a table before the place opens.

And when Michael pops each card into a street-corner mailbox or the mailbox in his motel lobby, or when he gives it to Mark or Arnie or Lenny or Emily to mail for him, I can feel our time together coming to an end, the sadness of saying good-bye and the hurt at the edge of missing him.

So for me, each card is like a different little movie—a movie starring Michael—a movie I can get lost in for a while.

Tonight, I decide, I'll get lost with Michael in Oswego.

It's my favorite.

Not the first card he sent from Oswego.

That's the one with the picture of Lake Ontario on it—the one where Michael fell asleep and ran off the road and woke up, unscratched, sitting in the middle of a corn field with his bumper nudged up against "a big old elm tree."

No, it's the second one that's my favorite—the one with the picture of the Oswego Theater on it.

It's the one where Sandy Shore called Michael and told him—on account of the accident—he was buying an old bus for the band to travel in. He was sending it to them along with a roadie named Jojo, who'd do all the driving from now on.

235

Sandy also said he'd charge the bus to the band's account but he'd take care of paying Jojo himself.

None of which is why the second postcard from Oswego is my favorite.

It's my favorite because of the part about Michael's working on my birthday song.

That's why it's my favorite.

That's why *Oswego II* is being featured at the *Magical Michael Film Festival* tonight.

As I start collecting up all the other postcards, making a small deck out of them, I remind myself—first thing tomorrow, I've got to get out my trusty Yellow Pages and start calling around to the stables they've got listed. Because the day I got the good news from J. B. Cooney—right after my big Unbirthday Party—I called Caroline to invite her up for the weekend.

She said she'd been waiting for me to call, but the first weekend she had free was—she looked in her calendar—and it turned out the first weekend she had free was this coming weekend.

Believe it or not, between then and now, Caroline has spent every single day either riding in a horse show or practicing to ride in a horse show or recovering from riding in a horse show.

So what does Caroline want to do when she finally gets up here?

Right.

She wants to go horseback riding.

I swear, Caroline's spent so much time around horses lately, when you ask her "How are you?" she just whinnies and tosses her head.

At least, that's what it seems like.

But anyway, she's coming up this weekend, and I promised her we'd do a lot of horsing around.

So that's first thing tomorrow.

As for tonight, I've stashed my deck of picture postcards in the pocket of my raincoat, which is hung in

236

the back of my closet, which is where I always stash them to keep them out of harm's way.

And I'm crawling into bed.

It's actually only about ten o'clock on a Thursday night, but I've been getting up with the sun, lately—when the world's still quiet and peaceful and when, if you're lucky, you can sometimes catch sight of a deer who's come down to the lake for a drink of water.

I know it sounds odd, but—up here, anyway—getting up with the sun and going to bed around ten at night seems right.

So I'm not embarrassed that it's only about ten o'clock.

I'm just going to turn out the light and watch *Michael Skye is Alive and Well and Playing in Oswego* one more time and then I'll call it a day.

Either that or answer the phone.

It's ringing, downstairs.

In the living room.

I think Bob's still down there, watching television.

Somebody's got it.

Somebody's climbing up the stairs.

Knocking on my door.

"Jessie? You awake?"

It's Bob.

"Yeah!" I answer, vaulting out of bed and opening the door.

"It's Elvis," he smiles.

"Michael!"

I dash for the stairs.

"Jess!"

I stop.

"Turn off the television when you're done," he says.

"Sure!" I tell him. "Okay. Thanks!"

Downstairs, a second later, I lift the phone and say, "I love you."

A girl laughs.

"Hang on a second," she says. "Hey, rock star—I got her!"

There's a party going on—music, loud voices and stuff.

I hear the phone clunk down on a table, somewhere in the middle of the party.

Michael's in Nantucket.

Which is this summer island off the coast of Massachusetts.

He wrote me.

He's playing in a club called FeeFee's.

But this sounds like a party at somebody's house.

"Jess?"

"Where are you?"

"At a farm," he says, shouting over the noise of the party.

"I thought farms were quiet," I tell him.

He laughs.

"Not this one," he says. "It belongs to the guy who owns the club. Pappalardi."

"Gesundheit!"

"Hey!" he shouts, "I got good news. That's what we're celebrating. That's why I'm calling."

"I can't hear you so good," I tell him.

I can't.

With all the noise.

"Hey, everybody!" he shouts. "Can you hold it down to a dull roar? For just a second?"

The answer's no.

A couple of people even shout it.

Somebody shouts something about a phone in another room and how Michael shouldn't hang up until she tells him to.

"Hang on, Jess," Michael tells me. "Jojo's got it worked out."

"Jojo?"

"Hang on," he says.

"Michael?" says this girl, picking up another phone,

somewhere in the house. She's the same girl I said "I love you" to a couple of seconds ago.

She's Jojo!

"Yeah?" says Michael.

"Hang up your end," she tells him, "and come into the bedroom."

"Okay," says Michael.

And he hangs up.

"Hi, Jess," says Jojo. "Did Michael tell you?"

"Are you Jojo the roadie?" I ask her.

She laughs.

"Among other things," she says.

"Oh," I say.

"Here's Michael," she says.

"She sounds cute," she tells Michael.

"Would you close the door?" Michael asks her.

"Lights on or off?" she asks him.

He doesn't answer.

She laughs.

"Thanks," he says.

"Jess?"

"Jojo's a girl."

"Yeah," he says. "Didn't I tell you?"

"Just that you had a roadie named Jojo, who drove the bus."

"Yeah, well—that's her."

"Why didn't you tell me?"

"I thought I did," he says. "It's no big deal. Sandy Shore just happens to be an Equal Opportunity Employer. And he also happens to dig Jojo's body. Get it?"

"Yeah," I tell him. "How old is she?"

"Jessie!"

"I'm sorry."

"So you want to hear the good news, or what?" he says.

"Good news."

"What are you doin' Saturday night?"

"I don't know," I tell him. "What?"

"Well," he says, "there's a town called Woodstock, about fifty miles away from you—according to Jojo, who knows about things like that."

"And there's this club in Woodstock called Fat City that's owned by this guy Red Weinrib . . .

"If I told you who Red Weinrib's managed over the years," he says, "it would sound so much like the Rock-and-Roll Hall of Fame, you wouldn't believe me. But anyway, Red wound up owning one of the big record companies and—even though he says he's 'retired' from the record business—Sandy says he's still the guy who calls the shots.

"Which means," says Michael, "if he wanted to—he could make The Skye Band happen. And—just to find out if he wants to—he's got The Skye Band playing at his place in Woodstock this Saturday night. For one show only.

"And guess who's going to be there?" he says.

"Me?"

"You got it!" he says. "I'll come and get you and I'll bring you back. As soon as I'm done with you."

"Michael!"

"I don't know the time or anything yet," he says. "Sandy's still got to get us out of a date in Framingham. But the guy in Framingham owes Sandy a favor, so it shouldn't be any sweat, he says. So as soon as I find out, I'll call you.

"You *can* make it, can't you?" Michael says.

"Sure," I tell him.

"Oh, Jess!" he says. "I've been looking forward to this."

"So have I," I tell him.

"It could be our big break."

"It will be."

"God, I've missed you."

"Me, too."

"See you soon."

"Good night, Michael."
"'Night, honey."
Eeeeeeeeeeegad!
I've never been so—
What am I?
Help!

Fifty–seven

The Oswego Theater.

It's the first thing I see when I wake up in the morning.

On the postcard Michael sent me.

The second one from Oswego.

My favorite.

Before I went to sleep last night, I propped it up against the lamp on the table next to my bed.

At the time, the way my brain was spinning—

Thinking about actually being with Michael again, and what he'd say, and what I'd say, and what he'd do and what I'd do—

Thinking about Caroline, and calling her and breaking our date, which happens to be the first date we've had since I broke our last date for our Farewell Lunch at The Station—

The way my brain was spinning—

I thought I'd better postpone the *Magical Michael*

Film Festival's showing of *Oswego II* until a more settled time.

"Which means," I tell myself now, looking over at the picture of the Oswego Theater, propped up on the table next to my bed, "it could be a while before I get a chance to see *Oswego II* again!"

Because the way it looks to me—as I pull back my blanket and crawl out of my lumpy little bed—the "more settled times" I'm waiting for could be a long time coming.

At least, I know—the way things are already jangling around in my head, when I've only been awake for a couple of seconds—these ain't them!

So—postponing this morning's tentatively scheduled screening of *Oswego II*—I pick up the postcard to carry it to the closet and stash it in my raincoat pocket.

It doesn't take that long to do, but while I'm doing it, while I've got the postcard in my hand, I can't resist taking a quick peek at *Oswego II*.

For inspiration.

. . . In a tacky motel room, stripped to the waist, his guitar in his lap, a pencil clenched between his teeth, Michael sits on top of a low dresser, working on a song.

Next to Michael, on top of the dresser, there's a sheet of motel stationery with a few words and chords scratched down on it, and a postcard, featuring a picture of the Oswego Theater.

The song Michael's working on isn't my birthday song. It's one of the newer, simpler songs Michael's been writing since he went out on the road. The crowds seem to like them better than some of Michael's older songs.

But now, Michael stops playing and looks over at the postcard with the picture of the Oswego Theater on it. He smiles and turns back to his guitar, and there it is—my birthday song.

So pretty—

But someone's at the door.

Mark.

He's heading into town for some breakfast. Does Michael want to come along?

Michael's got some writing to do.

Mark kids Michael about all work and no play making him a rich boy.

Michael laughs and asks Mark if he'd mind dropping something in a mailbox for him.

Mark wouldn't mind.

Michael shoves the postcard with the picture of the Oswego Theater on it into a motel envelope. He seals it, stamps it, scrawls my address across it and hands it to Mark.

Mark makes a crack about Michael's "love letters" and how he needs a pair of asbestos gloves to handle the one he's got in his hand.

Michael laughs and tosses Mark out of his room.

Michael—

That's it.

The postcard is stashed.

It's joined its friends in my raincoat pocket.

I wash and dress and head downstairs to join my friends in the kitchen.

It's time to break the news.

Bob and Lois take it pretty well.

Considering.

They don't like it, exactly, that I'm going to be seeing Michael this Saturday night.

They especially don't like that I have nothing to wear that Michael hasn't already seen a dozen times.

They don't like my breaking my date with Caroline, either.

But Bob doesn't say I can't go out with Michael.

And Lois doesn't mind driving me into Monticello to check out the stores for whatever I can find to wear that's not too expensive.

So they take it pretty well.

Considering.

Considering how badly Caroline takes it.

She understands how my seeing Michael comes first, and everything.

But she just doesn't understand why I couldn't tell her before now—when it's too late for her to enter the horse show she turned down because she was coming up here.

I try to explain.

But Caroline won't listen.

I invite Caroline to come up next weekend.

But she tells me to call her again when I'm sure I don't have plans for next weekend, too.

I promise her I will.

And I ask her to please understand.

She says she'll try.

But she's not making any promises.

That's how Caroline takes it.

Badly.

How do I take it?

That's what I'm still trying to figure out.

I'm sitting next to Lois—who is driving me into Monticello—and I'm trying to figure out how I really feel about seeing Michael again.

Excited, sure.

I feel very excited.

Wobbly about the knees and dizzy about the head and tingly just about everyplace else.

But—I have to admit it—I feel scared, too.

Of what Michael might be expecting me to do, for one thing.

And how he might look at me.

And act with me.

Now that we've made love.

And seen each other.

And touched each other.

And everything.

It's got to be different.

How he sees me.

245

And acts with me.
And what he expects me to do.
What does he expect me to do?
What do *I* expect me to do?
I don't want to think about it.
But I can't not think about it.
That's how I take it.
Scattered and confused.
With a fifty-percent chance of precipitation.

Fifty-eight

Shopping for clothes turns out to be a drag.

Largely because things a size up from my regular size fit me better than things my regular size do.

Largely.

I have been losing weight.

I had to.

The way I was going, I was headed straight for Junior Chubbies!

At least now I'm headed in the right direction.

But I still haven't arrived at my destination.

Which is pretty depressing.

And so—

After mucking through a bunch of crowded stores and changing in changing stalls that are too narrow to bend over in, and squeezing in and out of a half dozen pairs of pants—

I tell Lois I've changed my mind. I don't want to buy anything.

Everything is too expensive, I tell her. And what I've

got—since it's already stretched a little to accommodate my recent expansion—is good enough.

Lois has mixed feelings about my announcement. On the one hand, she likes not spending money. On the other hand, she's spent all this time and gone through all this hassle for nothing.

But she shakes it off.

A lot better than I would under the same circumstances, probably.

She's nicer than I am, Lois.

But I'm trying. So help me. I'm trying.

Anyway, Lois and I head back to White Lake and—when we get to the cottage, Grandma's waiting for me with a long face and a heavy message.

Michael called. He's not going to Woodstock. Not this weekend. Maybe later. He'll let me know as soon as he hears. I can't reach him anywhere because he's on the bus, traveling with the band. But he's sorry and he sends me his love.

I curse.

Four letters.

A word Lois has never heard me use.

"Well," she says, shaking her head and getting ready to offer me her sympathy or her advice.

I curse again.

The same word.

Then I say, "Excuse me."

And I turn and stomp off toward the lake.

Now I know what that J. Geils song is all about.

Love *does* stink!

I shout it—

"Love stinks!"

And then I shout the curse word.

I hope Matilda hears it.

And keels right over.

Thanks, Michael!

Thanks for everything!

Thanks a lot!

Fifty–nine

I thought about calling Caroline, of course.

Last night.

After I calmed down a little.

But I didn't really want to tell her about Michael breaking our date.

She might have laughed at me.

Or—even worse—she might have sympathized with me.

Also, I figured reinviting Caroline for the weekend I'd just disinvited her for, would be too much like adding insult to injury. It would probably just make her madder at me than she already was.

So I didn't do that, either.

In fact, all I did was—after dinner—I canceled the *Magical Michael Film Festival* ("Until Further Notice") and I turned out the light and I went to sleep.

That was it.

Until today.

And Avi.

Right.

The Israeli.

Excuse me.

The *Sabra!*

Now that I think about it, I'll bet it was Grandma who put him up to it.

She looked so sorry for me when she gave me Michael's message.

I'll bet she cooked up the whole thing as a way to cheer me up.

I wouldn't be surprised if Bob and Lois were in on it, too.

They were giving me the "Aw, poor baby!" treatment all last night.

Not in so many words.

But in the way I caught them looking at me, sometimes.

Yeah.

They were probably all in on it together.

It—

Saturday afternoon, I'm out in Grandma's garden, down on my hands and knees, picking the rocks out of the soil and tossing them into the tall grass, beyond the garden's edge.

It's not as bad as it sounds.

For one thing, I'm contributing a lot to the future happiness of some very deserving vegetable seeds.

With the rocks out of the soil, Grandma's vegetable seeds will be able to shoot their little roots down into the ground and pop their little stalks up into the air without anything getting in their way.

I imagine they'll be very grateful for my contribution.

So I can feel pretty good about that.

And tossing the rocks that I pull out of the soil into the tall grass at the edge of the garden has its pleasures, too.

For example, one of the rocks I throw almost hits Avi.

He was Grandma's idea.

I just know it now.

Although I didn't at the time.

All I knew at the time was, I heard the sound of a car or truck or something, and I looked up from this patch of soil I was working on, and there—bumping across the field, following the old wagon track—was one of these shiny, mile-high jeep things, with the big wheels and the roll-over bar.

I didn't know who it was at first.

And when I looked over at Grandma, she just gave me a kind of shrug.

Which—now that I think about it—was probably just a big act.

But anyway, I finally did recognize Avi, and I thought, *"Oh, no!"* and—hoping that he'd just disappear—I went right back to digging stones out of the soil and tossing them into the tall grass.

That's how I almost hit him.

"Hey!" he shouted. "Is that the way you greet a visitor?"

I told him I was sorry.

And then I went right back to pretending he wasn't there.

Which worked pretty well—at least, for a while— because Avi walked over to where Grandma was working, at the other end of the garden.

They talked a while, the two of them.

I tried not to listen, but that's hard to do when you're out in the country, in the middle of a big, open field and nothing else is going on.

Avi told Grandma she could improve the soil by plowing some lime into it.

He said the lime would balance out the acidity of the soil and improve the size and the quality of her vegetables.

251

He said if she would pay for the lime, he'd be glad to spread it over her garden and plow it into the ground for free.

Except, he said, when Grandma's vegetables came in, he might accept a few samples from her, if she insisted.

Grandma said, "Thank you," and she'd let him know.

And that's when my pretending wore out.

Because the next thing I knew, Avi was there, kneeling down next to me, working beside me, picking stones out of the soil and tossing them into the tall grass, right along with me.

He didn't say anything at all for a while.

But when he finally got around to it, he said he was sorry about coming on so strong the last time we met.

He said, in Israel, there were many beautiful girls and—since very few of them were shy like I am—Israeli boys got into the habit of coming on strong with them.

He said, when he first saw me, I was so beautiful, he thought for a moment he was back in Israel.

He forgot, he said, that in America, girls can be both beautiful and shy.

I told him it was all right.

I accepted his apology.

And I kept on digging up stones and tossing them into the tall grass.

He said, "I'd feel better—like you had really forgiven me, you know?—if you would go out with me to the movies tonight."

I almost laughed.

Because here he was, coming on strong all over again.

But he had this real sincere look on his face.

"What's playing?"

"Superman II."

I thought about it for a second.

Not much longer.

And I decided.

Why not?

So I told him, "Why not?"

Which is how—a few hours later—I came to find myself in the balcony of the Mountain Theater, fighting off the advances of the world's first strictly kosher Israeli octopus.

Avi—I swear—has as many hands as other people have fingers.

And, all through the movie, Avi's hands kept showing up in the most astonishing places.

I finally had to tell him to just cut it out!

And when he laughed, I got up from my seat and walked right out of the theater.

He caught up with me outside and he apologized again.

I asked him just where did he think he got off, pawing me over!

Who did he think he was?

Who did he think I was?

He asked me to calm down, and he said it was only because he liked me that he did those things.

If he didn't think I was very beautiful—

I told him I wasn't interested in his opinion.

Or his company.

Or his touching me.

And he'd better take me home.

Right now!

And he'd better not stop anywhere along the way.

And he'd better keep his hundred hands to himself.

And he said, shushing me, "Okay. Okay."

But as he drove me back to White Lake, he started working on me again.

Not physically, this time.

Mentally.

Which can be twice as bad.

He told me how disappointed he was that an Ameri-

253

can Jew like me could be so poisoned against a *Sabra* like him.

He had heard American Jews were anti-Semitic, he said, but this was the first time he'd ever run into it himself!

He felt hurt, he said, and angry, too.

He felt angry!

Like he's the *Old Testament* God's gift to women! *He* felt angry!

I felt so angry, I didn't even answer him!

Not until we pulled up to the cottage and I climbed down from his mile-high jeep.

When I got my feet planted back on the ground, I told him he might be right about me.

I told him, in my opinion, all *Sabras* were arrogant and obnoxious and devious creeps!

I also admitted that my opinion wasn't worth too much, since—so far—I'd only met one *Sabra*.

But—thanks to him—that might be enough *Sabras* to last me a lifetime!

Then I slammed his door as hard as I could.

And I stalked off toward the cottage.

When I arrived, I told everybody, yes, I had a fine time at the movies.

And no, I didn't think I'd be seeing Avi again.

I didn't tell them, "Nice try!"

Because, at the time, I hadn't figured out that they'd probably cooked the whole thing up as a way to get me out of my funk.

But now that I have figured it out, I'd have to admit it was a "try."

But "nice?"

"Nice," it definitely wasn't.

P.S.

All *Sabras,* please note—

I'm sure Avi is not typical of your average fantastic *Sabra,* so—from now on—I will dedicate

myself to overcoming whatever anti-*Sabra* preju-
dice I may have picked up from my unfortunate
encounters with him.

However—

Please do not call me.

I will call you.

Thank you.

Shalom,
Jessie Walters

Sixty

This week was three phone calls.

First, Sunday morning, I called Caroline to invite her up for this coming weekend.

She said she'd get back to me.

Then, Sunday night, Michael called from Framingham.

It turned out that the guy who owed Sandy a favor sold his club to a guy who didn't owe anybody any favors.

And this guy who didn't owe anybody any favors told Sandy something like, "I don't give a (*bleep*)! A deal's a deal! I don't give a (*bleep*) if the (*bleep*)ing President wants 'em to play in the (*bleep*)ing Flower Garden!"

Which is why Michael didn't go to Woodstock. And I didn't go to Woodstock. And why he called me from Framingham. Where he was working for this man who didn't owe anybody any favors. And probably never would.

Michael said he was real disappointed about our not

being together in Woodstock like we planned. But he said he wasn't too disappointed about not playing for Red Weinrib. Because Sandy Shore told him, "If Red Weinrib wants to hear you, he'll hear you. And soon. Don't worry about it."

Michael said he believed Sandy.

He said he was sure he'd be playing for Red Weinrib and we'd be together in Woodstock before long.

"Although," he said, "it's gonna seem like forever to me."

I told him, lately, every minute seemed like a million years to me.

And I love you.

And call me when you can.

And write me when you can't.

And we said good-bye.

And then, I called Caroline again.

Which is what I'm into at the moment, so I'd rather not dwell on Michael.

Caroline—

When she didn't call Monday or Tuesday or Wednesday, I swallowed my pride and I called her.

Wednesday night.

And we talked about it.

About everything.

Not too much about Michael.

Although I did have to tell her about how Woodstock got postponed and I didn't go, after all.

And—just like I was afraid of—she did have to tell me how sorry she was.

But that was about it for Michael.

We talked mostly about us.

And how we seemed to be going through a bad time together.

I told Caroline—if we got together—we might be able to put the bad times behind us and get back to being best friends to each other, like we used to be.

I told her I'd really like that.

And she said she would, too.

And she said—even though she was supposed to ride in a horse show this coming weekend—she had lots of horse shows to ride in, but she didn't have that many best friends. So she said she'd cancel out of the horse show and come up and visit me.

She accepted my invitation.

And I thanked her.

Sincerely.

I haven't got that many best friends, either.

And I'd really hate to lose Caroline.

Although—the way it looks at the moment—she's lost me.

It's Saturday afternoon, and we're riding horses at a stable somewhere outside Monticello.

Up until a little while ago, there were three of us riding together—Caroline and me and this woman who calls herself a *wrangler*.

This woman really knows the trails around here, and you can't go out riding—at least, not the first time— unless she goes riding along with you.

But the thing is, this woman happens to be a real good rider.

And as soon as she saw that Caroline was a good rider, too, she started challenging her—to see who was braver, who'd ride faster through thicker clumps of trees, who'd jump higher over fallen logs and other horsy stuff like that.

And since Caroline is not about to take a back seat to anybody when it comes to horseback riding, she took this woman up on her challenge, and—about five minutes ago—the two of them went charging off.

Which left me, bringing up the rear.

Which—considering the current size of my rear—is no easy thing to bring up.

Especially in polite conversation.

The thing is—

I can ride a horse.

I'm not crazy about it.

But I can do it.

I just can't do it very well.

Especially the part where you're supposed to lift your rear up off the saddle when the horse's middle sags, and rest it down on the saddle when the horse's middle arches back up to meet you.

I can never get the timing of that just right.

So riding a horse for me is sort of like an upside-down version of getting spanked with a saddle.

And it hurts.

During.

And especially after.

I'd give it up completely.

If it wasn't such jolly good fun—ho! ho!

And if it wasn't for Caroline.

Who is currently crashing through the woods somewhere, way up ahead of me.

I'll bet she's giving the lady wrangler a run for her money, too.

Or—to be more specific—a run for *my* money.

Or—to be perfectly honest—a run for *Lois*'s money.

Because it's my treat, this weekend.

All of it.

Except the bus fare, which Caroline already paid herself.

The rest is my treat.

Some treat!

"Whoa!"

It works!

My horse stops.

His name is Molasses, because he's so slow and so sweet.

I think he's glad to stop.

I know I am.

Because I've just had an accident.

What you might call a happy accident.

Right.

My unpunctuated sentence.

It's punctuating itself.

Right now.

Right here.

Tah-dah!

Bless you, Mother Nature!

Welcome back, Old Friend!

You don't know how much I missed you!

On the other hand—now that it's Punctuation Day—I've got a problem on my hands.

What I've got to do now is tell Molasses, "Let's you and me turn around and go back the way we came. Let's go back to the barn. Where all your nice horsy friends are. Where all the nice, tasty hay is waiting!"

The thing is, I have to figure out a way to say that in Horse Language.

But the best I can do is broken Horse Language.

I pull back—gently but firmly—on Molasses's right rein and I whisper in his ear, "Soup's on!"

It works.

Thank goodness!

Maybe because I've spoken broken Horse Language to a broken-down horse.

I don't know.

But by the time Caroline comes galloping up to the barn, about a half hour later—

After I've paid a quick visit to the dispenser in the Ladies' Room—

The sign on the door says "Mares"—

I'm pretty much together.

And feeling a lot like my old self again.

"Where's Butch Cassidy?" I ask Caroline as she leads her horse into the barn.

"She's okay," Caroline smiles. "She just pulled up at the creek I jumped over."

Caroline pats her horse's neck.

"I guess she thought it would be safer to walk her horse around," she says.

Caroline's so pleased with herself, I can't help but laugh.

And, blushing a little, Caroline joins in with me.

"What happened to you?" she asks, giving her horse over to the stableboy.

It comes to me.

Right on the spot.

How can I tell Caroline what I'm not, without telling her exactly why I'm not what I'm not.

How I can turn my happy accident into an Immaculate Misconception.

Acting a little embarrassed, I tell Caroline, "I've had an accident."

"You fell?" she says.

"No," I tell her. "Not that kind of accident."

"What kind?"

"I broke something."

She doesn't understand.

"Something—down there."

Her eyes go wide.

"Jessie!"

"It's okay," I tell her. "It didn't hurt. Much."

"Jessie!"

"Well," I tell her, heaving a philosophical sigh, "I guess it had to happen, sooner or later."

"Yeah," she says. "One way or another!"

"Yeah," I agree. "Although this wasn't exactly the way I had in mind."

"You mean," she says, "you and Molasses? It wasn't a meaningful relationship?"

That does it.

I mean, Caroline, of all people!

Caroline, who almost never tells jokes.

Who'd expect Caroline to come up with me and Molasses not having a meaningful relationship?

It cracks me up.

And Caroline, too.

On the other hand, if Caroline didn't come up with a joke like that, who else in the world would?

Nobody.

So we're both laughing our heads off—and I'm thinking how lucky I am to have my funny best friend Caroline around again—when Butch Cassidy comes riding in and jumps down from her horse.

I guess she thinks we're laughing at her.

Because, right away, she starts yelling at Caroline—about taking chances, about endangering her horse, about how Caroline would be responsible if anything happened to her horse, and on and on.

Caroline and I don't answer her.

We just look at each other and pick up laughing where we left off, and turn and walk away.

We hitchhike into Monticello.

Actually, we don't hitchhike.

We grab a ride with a truck that's just pulling out onto the road as we walk up to it.

We've decided that the thing to do about my happy accident is to celebrate it.

With ice cream sundaes.

The hell with Size 5!

There's this ice cream parlor in Monticello that just happened to catch my eye when I was looking for something to wear to—

Anyway—

I thought this would be a good time to check it out.

This ice cream parlor.

Caroline agreed.

Although she wasn't too sure about the hitchhiking part.

Which is why the truck pulling out onto the road

when we got there was a real break for all of us ice cream fiends.

So—

Caroline and I are sitting in this ice cream parlor in Monticello.

It's about fifteen minutes later.

We've got these huge ice cream sundaes sitting in front of us.

And these two guys checking us out from the booth across the way.

Oh!

Lois!

I called her to tell her she shouldn't pick us up at the stable because we got offered a lift into Monticello.

So she's coming for us here.

But these two guys—

I guess they're about fourteen or fifteen or somewhere in there.

Neither of them is any big threat to become a movie star or anything.

But they look nice enough.

Caroline and I are pretending we don't notice them checking us out.

But it's pretty obvious they're discussing which one of them is going to make the move on us.

Now, I guess they've decided.

The tallish guy with the straight red hair is standing up.

He'll go first, and his shorter friend with the curly brown hair will follow along, just a little behind him.

"Excuse me," says Straight Red. "Are you girls from around here? Because we're not. And we thought you might be able to tell us, you know, what's going on. Like, where everybody hangs out and all."

Caroline thinks Straight Red's cute.

I can tell.

By the way she's not looking at him.

"Where are you from?" I ask Straight Red.

"I'm from New Haven, Connecticut," says Curly Brown, piping up from the background. "And he's from White Lake."

Which makes me laugh.

Which makes Straight Red turn to Curly Brown and say, "Mike!"

That's his name.

Short for Michael, I'm sure.

There's no getting away from him!

"I'm Caroline," says Caroline, holding out her hand to Straight Red.

"Allen," he says, smiling and taking her hand and giving it a shake.

Allen drops into the booth beside me.

"I'm Mike," says Mike, shaking my hand and dropping into the booth next to Caroline.

"Jessie."

"There's a place called Milo's," Allen says. "They have live rock bands every night. They check I.D.s. But the guy at the door went to school with my brother."

"Imagine," I tell Caroline, "he just got in from White Lake and he already knows the guy who watches the door at Milo's."

"Magnetic personality," Caroline guesses.

"You want to go?" Mike asks me.

"When?" Caroline asks Allen.

"Now," he smiles. "Tonight."

"We can't," I remind Caroline.

My parents have people coming up from Jersey, and there's going to be a big party at the cottage.

"Oh, yeah," Caroline sighs.

"Maybe next week," she tells Allen.

I'm amazed!

I mean, it's all right.

264

It's even more than all right.

It's terrific!

But I haven't invited Caroline to come up next weekend.

Caroline's just invited herself.

Because she's making a pass at Straight Red.

Caroline!

Who used to blush if a boy even said hello to her.

Caroline!

Maybe there's something to this horse stuff, after all.

"What about you?" Mike asks me. "What are you doing next weekend?"

"I'm engaged to a United States Marine," I tell him.

"Oh," he says.

He isn't sure if he should take me seriously, or what.

"Where's your ring?" he asks me.

"I wear it around my neck," I tell him.

"Ring around the collar," says Allen.

Caroline laughs.

"How do I reach you before next weekend?" Allen asks Caroline.

"You could call *her*," says Caroline, nodding to me. "I'm just up for the weekend. This weekend and next."

Which is how I happen to be writing my White Lake phone number on a paper napkin when Lois walks in.

"Gotta go," I say, jumping up. "Hi, Mom!"

"Hi," she says. She looks surprised—and delighted—to see Caroline and especially me, sitting with a couple of younger-than-Michael-aged boys.

Caroline and I tell Allen and Mike good-bye.

"I'm pretty sure I'll be up here again, next weekend," Caroline tells Allen, shaking his hand good-bye.

"She's definitely sure," I tell him.

"I'll call—ah—"

"Jessie," Mike reminds him.

"Yeah," says Allen, smiling at me. "Jessie."

I can't tell you how nice it is—

Seeing Caroline reaching out for what she wants.

Instead of shyly waiting and secretly hoping for what she wants to happen to her.

I don't know if it was riding in all the horse shows that did it.

Or standing up to Butch Cassidy.

Or hearing "The Legend of Me and Molasses."

I don't know what's got Caroline acting like a person who knows what she wants and isn't afraid to reach out and grab it.

But whatever it is, I like it.

And I like her for finding it, wherever she found it, and for knowing that it's something she ought to try on for size, whatever the consequences.

I like it and I like her.

She's catching up with me.

In fact, she might even be ahead of me.

Not in what she does.

But in how she feels about herself.

In how she insists on feeling about herself.

I'm impressed.

Although I'm not so sure she should have tested out her new reach-out-and-grab-it philosophy on Allen.

Still, it's the principal of the thing.

And Caroline's got hold of it.

She's exactly as terrific as I always thought she was.

And I'm really sorry, the next night, when I have to say good-bye to Caroline at the bus station in Monticello.

She reminds me that I'm going to call her as soon as I hear from Allen.

I promise her I will. And I hug her good-bye. And I put her on the bus.

And as the bus pulls out—carrying Caroline back to Horse-Show Heaven—I stand at the loading dock and wave good-bye.

Sixty—one

That night—Sunday night—Michael calls.

Woodstock is "on" again.

This time it's for sure.

Next weekend.

Saturday night.

"You'll be able to make it, won't you?" he says.

Biting the bullet, I tell him, "Yup!

"I can't wait," I tell him.

"I'll call you again when we can work out the time and everything," he says.

"One show?" I ask him.

"Yeah," he says.

"Good," I say.

"Yeah," he says. "That'll give us some time to ourselves."

"That's what I was thinking," I tell him.

"Soon, honey," he says.

" 'Night," I tell him.

" 'Night, Jess," he says.

So that's what I'm thinking about—nervously—about Michael, and going to Woodstock with him, and being in Woodstock with him, and coming home from Woodstock with him—when the phone rings again.

"It's been canceled!" I think.

But this time, it isn't Michael.

This time, it's Allen!

Calling to find out just when, next weekend, Caroline is coming up to visit.

Ow!

I've done it again!

I've screwed up Caroline's plans for the weekend.

Incredible!

"There's a problem," I tell Allen. "I'm not sure Caroline's actually coming up next weekend. Because of this thing that's come up."

"Oh," he says, sounding disappointed.

"Maybe we can work something out," I tell him. "I'll have to talk to her, though."

"Okay," he says. "But if she's not coming up . . ."

"Yeah?"

"Well," he says, "you know, I really do admire you for how you're being so loyal to a United States Marine and all, but—"

Interrupting, I tell Allen how very much I appreciate his admiration.

And because I don't want to lose his admiration—

And because I really love my best friend, Caroline—

I promise him I'll tell Caroline he called.

And meanwhile, I tell him, I'd appreciate it if he'd *stuff it!*

Sixty-two

I didn't want to tell Caroline about what a rat Allen was and how—when he thought she might not be coming up this weekend—he started leading up to asking me out.

I mean, after she'd gone out on a limb for him like she did, I thought it would break her heart to know that—at the first opportunity—Allen had proven himself to be a Certified Public Rat.

I also didn't feel much like telling Caroline that I'd made another date with Michael and that the date was for this coming weekend, when she was planning to be with her rat friend, Allen.

But what I did—the next day, around dinnertime, when I figured Caroline would be home—is I called her and told her everything.

Because she's my best friend.

And you owe it to your best friends to tell them the truth.

About everything.

Except for me and Michael making love, and me thinking I was pregnant, and all that.

Which is nobody's business.

But mine.

And Michael's.

But when I told Caroline everything—just the way it happened—she didn't say thank you, right away.

I didn't really expect her to.

She was hurt about Allen, like I knew she would be.

And she wanted to know if I was sure Allen was really leading up to asking me out.

I told her I was pretty sure, or else I wouldn't have said to him what I did.

"I'm sorry, Caroline," I told her. "But Allen's a rat."

"I think I suspected it," she sighed. "When he said he was from out of town but he was really from White Lake."

"I'm sorry, Caroline," I told her.

"What can you do?" she said. "A rat's a rat. And that's all there is to that."

"Poetry!" I told her.

She laughed.

I told her—if she wouldn't miss me Saturday night—she was welcome to come up and check out her rat friend for herself.

"No," she said. "I'll take your word for it. And Jess—?"

"Yeah?"

"Thanks for telling me."

"You're welcome."

"Will you call me Sunday?" she asked. "And tell me all about your date with Michael?"

"*All* about it?" I asked her.

"Well," she said, "as much as you can tell me without making me blush."

I laughed.

And I told her I'd call.

And we said good night.

Me and my best friend—

Caroline

Sixty-three

When Michael's really serious about something—like when he's writing a song, for instance—he gets this expression on his face that reminds me of a parked car.

An empty one.

One that's just sitting there, waiting calmly, while its driver is off somewhere, taking care of some very important business.

Why I mention this is—when I heard Michael's car pulling in and I went out to greet him—I could see he was really glad to see me. But just beneath Michael's smile I could see the silhouette of this parked car.

It's been there ever since.

Maybe he's thinking about tonight.

Maybe he's nervous about it.

"What time should we expect Jessie home?" Bob asks Michael—smiling and trying to sound like he's just curious, and not really concerned.

"About two or two-thirty," Michael guesses.

"Mm," says Bob, nodding his head and thinking it over.

He looks at me, considers, and makes up his mind.

Turning to Michael, he nods and says, "Okay. Two-thirty. But no later!"

"Bob!" I think.

"What are you doing?

"Where is this 'Stern-Father' Act coming from, all of a sudden?"

"Yes, sir," says Michael, taking it right in stride. "Good night."

He nods to Lois.

"Good night, Mrs. Walters."

"Good luck," she tells him.

"Yeah," says Bob, returning—momentarily—from Stern-Fatherland. "Good luck tonight."

"Thanks," says Michael.

Lois hugs me and says, "Have a good time."

"I will," I tell her.

I give Bob a hug.

"Good night, Dad."

"Two-thirty," he says.

Not to me.

To Michael!

Michael nods his head and says, "Well—"

And we're out the door, and heading for Woodstock.

"How come you've still got your wagon?"

We're heading up the path to where Michael's parked.

"Oh," Michael smiles. "I persuaded Jojo—Wait 'til you meet her. She's a real pistol—But seven people living out of one bus that you don't want to take everywhere just doesn't make much sense. It kind of limits your mobility, you know? And anyway, I didn't want some stranger hot-rodding my wagon back to New Jersey for me. It's been too good to me."

"Like a cowboy loves his horse," I tell him.

274

He smiles and nods back toward the cottage and says, "Love me, don't they?"

"Doesn't everybody?" I ask him.

He looks at me for a long second.

Thinking about it.

Then he laughs and shakes his head and puts his arm around my waist.

"I've missed you," he says.

"You don't know!" I tell him.

He smiles his smile—warm and slow.

And for a second I feel like I'm home again.

Sixty-four

"Are you nervous about tonight?"

It's about twenty minutes later, and Michael and I are heading north out of Monticello on Route 42, and—even though we've been talking about this and that all along the way—we haven't gotten around to talking about the parked car under Michael's smile yet.

Not until now.

"It's not really tonight I'm worried about," he says. "It's forever."

I ask him what he means.

He doesn't answer right away.

Then he says, "It's like when you first start playing. I was about twelve when I first started. Playing in little groups. In guys' cellars and garages and stuff.

"I wasn't real good. But I liked it. And I kept at it. And I got better, the more I kept at it.

"And someplace in there—probably the first time I got paid cash money for making music—I started imagining how it might be—how my life might be—if I

276

could actually make a living at it. At making music. You know what I mean?"

"I think so," I tell him.

"Maybe," he says. "Maybe you do. But now—now, it's just starting to look like I might be able to actually live the life that I imagined myself living, way back then. Do you know how scary that is?"

I shake my head.

I can't imagine it.

Not really.

It's never really come up in my life.

Or in the lives of my friends.

I guess it could be scary.

"There's something about it," Michael says. "I've got this feeling that I left something out of it. I don't know what it is. But back when I was imagining this life for myself—I've got a feeling there was something I forgot to put into it. Something important. Something I'm gonna hate to be without if I actually let myself go for it and I wind up getting the life I imagined—just the way I imagined it—way back then.

"Do you know what I'm saying? Or do you just think I'm nervous about tonight?" he asks me.

"I think I know what you're saying," I tell him. "And I know you're definitely nervous about tonight."

He smiles and reaches his hand over and rests it on my leg, just above my knee.

"Michael!"

"I'm glad you're here, Jess."

"I'm glad I'm here, too," I tell him, lifting his hand from my leg and placing it back on the steering wheel. "But I'd still like to get there—in one piece, if possible."

He laughs.

And I'm in love with him, all over again.

Or still.

But it's different, how I feel toward him.

I don't know what it is.

Maybe it's because we've made love.

Or maybe it's all the changes I went through when I was worried about being pregnant.

Or maybe, from all the postcards he's written me and all the time that's passed, I know him better and understand him differently than I used to.

Maybe I know me better and understand me differently than I used to.

Like I said, I don't know what it is.

But for the first time, really, I feel like taking Michael in my arms and holding him and telling him, "It's going to be all right, Michael. It is. You'll see. . . ."

I push over next to Michael and rest my hand on his leg, just above his knee.

He smiles and puts his arm around me.

"Michael!" I remind him.

"Don't worry," he smiles. "I've had years of practice."

I laugh.

And kiss his cheek.

And he says, "Easy, girl!"

And I smile.

And he laughs.

And right now—looking at him laughing—I can't see a trace of the parked car, anywhere.

Sixty-five

When we arrive where the band is staying in Woodstock—at this geodesic dome that Sandy Shore's borrowed from some friends of his—there's a big barbecue going on.

"Jojo's idea," Michael tells me as we pull up onto the shoulder of the car-clogged driveway.

"Is there anybody here I know?" I ask Michael as I climb out of the car.

"Jessie!" shouts Mark.

"Hey, Jess!" calls Arnie.

"Jessie's here!" shouts Emily.

"Guess so," says Michael, smiling at me over the hood of the car and reaching his hand out to me.

I take his hand, and we walk into the crowd.

Everybody in the band acts real glad to see me—like I'm a long-lost member of the family, or something.

And I'm real glad to see them, too.

But aside from them and Michael, everybody else at the barbecue—mostly pretty girls in jeans and blouses and people who look like musicians or roadies and a couple of older business types, maybe twenty-five people in all—everybody else I see is a stranger.

And they're all just kind of standing around the yard, holding paper plates filled with hot dogs and hamburgers, and drinking beer, and smoking dope, and trying to talk over the music that's blasting out through the open doors of the dome.

"Jojo!" Michael calls.

She's working over an outdoor grill built out of bricks.

Jojo looks like she's built out of bricks, too.

"Tough" is the word.

Not hard.

But too-gether!

There's not a sliver of extra weight on her long, lean body, and the jeans she's wearing under her juice-splattered apron look like a layer of smooth denim skin.

Jojo's hair is long and blond, and she wears it loose, so she can toss it aside and reveal her Siamese-cat smile before she spots me standing next to Michael and says, "Jessie!"

"Hi!" I say, nodding my head and giving her my party smile.

She's about twenty-five, I guess.

Maybe less.

And she doesn't look anything like any roadie I ever heard of.

But then—now that I think about it—I haven't really heard about all that many roadies.

But anyway, Jojo's nice and friendly and she's cute, like a big sister, with Michael.

And she's nice enough to warn me that I'd better fill up on the hot dogs and hamburgers because "You don't know what bad food tastes like until you've eaten at Fat City."

Just to be friendly—or at least not to be unfriendly—I take a heaping plate of charred meat and blackened buns and potato salad and stuff and—moving along with Michael—I carry it into the dome.

Being inside a dome is like being inside the top half of a translucent golf ball.

It's like a giant cave—one big room with a high, curving see-through ceiling that curves right down to the ground.

Except for the bathroom.

Which is this separate little box with a door that they would have wedged into a corner, if there was a corner in a geodesic dome.

Michael and I find a spot to squat and eat our dinners.

The reason I say "squat" is, the spot we find is one of those beanbag couches, where it's hard enough balancing yourself on the chair, without having to balance your paper plate on your lap.

But we manage, somehow.

Michael and I.

And while we're eating and letting all the music and bustle wash right over us, people start dropping by.

Just about everybody in the band—at one time or another—drops by and shouts "Hi!" or "How's it goin'?" or whatever.

And a lot of strangers—who turn out to be friends of Michael's or friends of friends of Michael's—drop by, too.

It's like Michael's a magnet that everybody's drawn to.

Especially me.

Especially now—

Trading smiles with him like we both know a terrific joke that no one else has ever heard.

Sliding closer together.

Touching shoulders.

Hips.

Thighs.

It's like it was.

In the beginning.

When we first started out.

Sweet.

And warm.

And tender.

And then—in what seems like no time at all—the music is over and everybody's gone.

Everybody but the family, I mean—the band, the guys and their girls, Emily and her friend, Michael and me.

And Jojo.

"I'll be back for y'all around seven thirty," she announces. "If you're lookin' for a good time, don't keep me waiting!"

Which—plus the way she tosses her hair and struts out the door—gets her a big round of cheers and whistles from all the guys.

Except for Michael.

His voice soft and low and husky, his eyes loving me, the way they used to, he says, "Come on."

He leads me over to this pile of rolled-up sleeping bags.

"Gotta make do," he smiles.

Picking one out, he leads me over to this spot where the sun is shining down through the tops of the trees and the skin of the dome.

And he spreads the sleeping bag out over the carpeted floor, and we crawl inside it.

He takes me in his arms and holds me and kisses me.

Sweetly.

And he's the old Michael again.

The Michael I'll always love.

"If it's okay with you," he whispers, kind of apologizing to me, "I'd like to rest up now and party after the show. Okay?"

I smile and kiss him.

Sweetly.

The way he kissed me.

Only a little longer.

A little deeper.

Michael smiles and closes his eyes and falls asleep.

Just like that.

I lie in his arms, with my head on his shoulder, rising and falling with his breathing.

With my eyes closed, I can feel the smile on my face, as—after a moment—I fall fast asleep, too.

We wake to the beeping of a horn.

The bus is here.

"Rise and shine!" she calls, strutting through the door and flicking on the stereo and all the lights.

"Aw!"

"Jojo!"

"Our public needs us!" shouts Leroy, rallying the troops from their various out-in-the-open hideaways.

"Our public," says Arnie, "needs a good stiff—!"

"Stiff drink," says Jojo. "So do I. Let's go!"

"Jojo?"

Michael looks up at her from down on the floor, where we're still lying together.

Talking softly, he asks her, "You got anything?"

She smiles.

"I've got everything!" she says.

"I know," Michael laughs. "But—"

"Is she cool?" Jojo asks, nodding at me.

"Jess," says Michael, "I'll be right back."

As he starts climbing out of our sleeping bag, I ask him, "Where you going?"

"I've got to talk to Jojo," he says. "I'll just be a second."

He kisses me and heads off toward the bathroom with Jojo.

Now, following Jojo into the bathroom, Michael closes the door behind him.

I keep my eyes on the door.

After a few seconds, it opens, and out comes Michael, smiling and looking refreshed.

Like he just stepped out of the shower.

Except he isn't wet.

Jojo doesn't come out of the bathroom.

Arnie goes in.

The door closes.

A few seconds pass.

The door opens.

Out comes Arnie, smiling and looking refreshed.

Emily's next.

She goes into the bathroom.

Closes the door.

"What's going on in there?" I ask Michael.

"Wake-up ceremony," Michael explains. "The Reverend Jojo Martindale presiding."

"Oh," I say, laughing along with him like I know what he's talking about.

I'll find out later.

Or sometime.

Or never.

I love Michael.

Again.

Or still.

So what do I care?

284

Sixty-six

"No, thanks," says Michael.

We're sitting in the band's dressing room, backstage at Fat City, and Michael's telling Jojo he'd rather not take a hit from the bottle of Southern Comfort she's offering him.

"Good for what ails you," she says.

"I'm not ailing," says Michael, smiling and looking over at me.

Jojo laughs.

"Haven't you heard, Michael?" she says. "Everybody's ailing."

"Okay! He's here!" Sandy Shore announces, darting in the door. "Sorry, everybody! I gotta talk to the boys."

I kiss Michael.

For luck.

"Everybody's going to be sitting together," Sandy announces. "So behave yourselves. And yock it up!"

Which, for some reason—maybe because it's so

corny—makes Michael laugh. And once Michael starts, everybody follows.

And that's how I leave them.

Laughing.

I walk out of the dressing room and through the kitchen and into the club.

Except for Red Weinrib, there's nothing real unusual about Fat City.

Except for Red Weinrib and the jug band they've got playing, up on the stage.

A jug band is a very unusual thing.

It's an old-fashioned orchestra, made up of a clarinet and a violin and a harmonica and, among other things, two people who contribute to the music by blowing into the tops of these big old clay jugs.

Like they keep whiskey in.

The kind you have to hoist over your shoulder if you want to pour yourself a drink.

It's like blowing across the tops of Coke bottles, what these people are doing. Except they're making music. Nice tubby, jolly music.

But—you've got to admit it—jug bands are very unusual.

Which—now that I'm headed straight for his table—Red Weinrib is, too.

At least, he looks it.

He's a three-hundred-pound, long-haired and bearded, sixty-year-old, chubby-cheeked millionaire hippie, who doesn't just look like he could eat you for breakfast—he looks like he already has.

"Hi," I say, taking a seat at his table.

I'm not the first, I'm happy to say.

There are other people—from the dressing room and the barbecue—already sitting at the table when I arrive.

"Mmph," says Mr. Weinrib, returning my greeting.

"Hah!" says this beautiful red-haired woman—who

is about a third of his age and a quarter of his weight—and who is sitting practically on top of him.

"Get you something?"

The waiter.

Being pleasant.

The customer.

Being nonchalant.

"Coke."

"Expensive habit!" says Weinrib, shaking his finger at me and laughing.

"Make it a double!" says his red-haired playmate.

Weinrib laughs.

"Make it a triple!" I tell the waiter.

Stopping the laughter.

Dead.

Except for my own.

Which hangs there.

"Sandy!"

Just in the nick of time, my Short White Knight, Sandy Shore, comes riding to my emotional rescue.

"Red! Phyllis! The boys are all set. How you doin' since lunch?"

"They ready?" says Weinrib.

"They're gold!" says Sandy.

Weinrib laughs.

The crowd applauds.

The jug band's done.

It doesn't take long to break down a jug band's basic equipment.

And with Jojo in charge, it doesn't take long for the tech crew to set up the equipment for the Skye Band.

Good luck, Michael. I hope you get what you want!

"Friends of Fat City," says the announcer. "We want you to meet some new friends. Say hello to Michael Skye and The Skye Band!"

They're different!

That's the first thing that hits me.

For one thing, they don't come out roarin' and smokin' and trying to blow everybody's house down.

They come out like they know they're good.

And they aren't kidding around.

And—if you've got any ears at all—you'll pick up on what they're doing.

And—if you don't have ears—why should they waste their time trying to talk to you?

And what they're doing—the songs they're doing and the way they're doing them—is different, too.

Everything's a lot simpler and clearer now.

So—instead of thinking about the song so much, you think more about the singer and the way he's singing.

And—since the singer happens to be Magical Michael Skye—what you get is pretty fantastic.

All the riveting energy is still there.

In Michael's singing and the way he plays and the way he moves.

But Michael's doing more than putting out energy now.

He's controlling it.

Playing with it.

He's playing with the energy like he was playing with a lion on a leash.

And you can't take your eyes off him.

You don't dare not listen to him for even one second.

You're afraid if you do, you'll miss something.

Something that will happen once and never happen again.

Because Michael Skye doesn't bowl you over anymore.

Now, Michael Skye blows you out!

He's incredible!

And his new songs are incredible, too.

Because of how different they are from what they used to be.

Michael doesn't write about Happiness anymore.

He doesn't write about Sadness.

The way Michael writes now, they're all mixed up together—with little bits of happiness stuck in big chunks of sadness, like chocolate chips in cardboard cookies.

Michael's songs celebrate the little bits of happiness.

Or they complain about how hard they are to come by.

Or they mourn over how much you have to pay for the few you get.

Together, Michael's new songs make up a world of their own.

A dark but possible world.

A world where Michael Skye is King.

And that's how the audience—the crowd—reacts to him.

To Michael.

Like, he's a king who's come to shed his light on their dark but possible world.

They greet him with cheers.

They shout his praises.

And by the time Michael's halfway through his first encore, they're up on their feet, stomping out the time and showering him with their love.

Red Weinrib doesn't leave his seat.

Red Weinrib doesn't get to his feet lightly.

And anyway, Red Weinrib's having much too good a time, just sitting in his chair—letting red-haired Phyllis do the dancing, up on her feet and pressing against him.

And then, it's over.

The place is a madhouse.

And then, we're all back in the dressing room, sitting around and waiting to hear the verdict.

And finally—

Sandy walks in.

Looking very happy.

"Loved you!" he announces.

And everybody whoops and shouts!

And Sandy hugs Michael.

And me.

And everybody.

"So now what?" says Mark.

And everybody laughs.

"Now," says Sandy, "we get down to business. Mr. Weinrib. And Mr. Shore. And your leader, Mr. Skye. In person. At Weinrib's house. In half an hour."

Everybody whoops and shouts.

Except for me.

I mean, I'm really happy for everybody.

Except for me.

Not so much because I haven't been invited to Weinrib's house.

More because I don't belong in Michael's world.

Not anymore.

And I know it.

I hate it.

But I know it.

And I know there's nothing I can do.

"Think you can make it?" Sandy asks Michael.

And the room goes quiet.

Michael looks at Mark.

And Arnie.

And Emily.

And Leroy.

And Lenny.

And Sandy.

Then, he looks at me and gives me this devilish smile and—like he's inviting the whole world into our bedroom—he asks me, "Can I make it?"

If everybody didn't laugh, I'd probably cry.

But I don't.

I throw myself into Michael's arms and hug him and hide my face against his chest.

He hugs me back and then, looking down and seeing the expression on my face, he gets real serious and apologetic.

"Just joking around," he says.

"I know," I tell him.

I do.

He didn't mean any harm.

He's just happy.

And he should be.

He's almost got what he wants.

The life he imagined for himself.

Way back when.

And he knows it isn't me that he left out of the life he imagined for himself, way back when.

Because Michael didn't leave me out of his life, until—

When was it?

When he left home and went out on the road?

When he started writing his new songs?

When he started believing in them?

When the crowds started loving him?

When I did?

"It's, uh—" says Sandy, standing at Michael's shoulder, squeezing a word in edgewise.

"It's—uh—liable to be a late night," he says.

"A couple of hours?" Michael asks him.

Sandy shrugs.

"With this kind of thing? With these kind of people? Open-ended," he says.

And he stifles a laugh.

"Excuse the language," he tells me.

He tells Michael, "You gotta keep it loose."

And he stifles another laugh.

And he claps Michael on the shoulder and reminds him, "Half hour!" and darts away.

Michael looks at me.

"I don't have to—"

"Don't be silly," I tell him.

"Aw, Jess!" he says, hugging me. "I didn't know it was going to work out like this."

"How could you?"

"I'm sorry," he says.

"If you want me to," says Mark, dropping in on us, "I'll drive Jessie home."

Michael looks at him.

He looks back at me.

"I think you'd better," he tells Mark, and, shaking his head, he tells me, "There's no telling how long—"

"I understand," I tell him.

I wish I didn't.

But I think—at last—I do.

"Whenever you like," says Mark.

"Now," I tell him.

"I'll come see you tomorrow," Michael promises me.

"Good luck," I tell him, kissing him good-bye.

"Thanks for coming," he says.

"Good luck," Mark tells Michael.

Without looking at Mark—without taking his eyes off me—Michael says, "Thanks."

Sixty-seven

Mark—who usually doesn't have much to say—has plenty to say.

All the way back to White Lake.

He's behind the wheel of Michael's wagon.

And I'm sitting over on the passenger side of the front seat, propped in the corner, between the seat and the door.

And he's telling me how, right now, it seems to him like everything he's been through while he was trying to make himself a musician was worth it.

Like all of it—

Even the worst of it—

It all had something to teach him before he could go on and get to tonight.

It's like—for once—the whole thing, his whole life, makes some kind of sense to him.

Michael—

Sandy Shore—

Finally, Mark's gotten to the right place at the right

time with the right goods and the right kind of people—the best kind of people, friends—all around him, watching his back, taking care of him.

It's fantastic!

He can't believe it!

And he can't believe I'm crying, either.

"Happiness?" he asks me.

I keep my eyes on the road.

And shake my head.

And hold my silence.

"I've never seen him better," he says.

I nod my head.

"He knows what he's doing now," he says. "He's taking responsibility for what he's doing."

I know.

I nod my head.

To tell Mark I know.

"I'm sorry, Mark," I apologize. "I know it's a wonderful night for you. But—"

"You and Michael going through something?" he guesses.

"Yeah," I tell him. "I'm sorry. I know it isn't fair."

"Hell!" he laughs, smiling over at me, looking as happy as I've ever seen him and probably as happy as he's ever been.

"You don't have to worry about me," he says. "I've got so much goin' right now, they should wire me up to the next five space shots. I could toss those suckers out there like I was flickin' away cigarettes!"

And I have to laugh.

Even though there's nothing funny about it.

About Michael and me.

And how it's never going to work out.

However much we want it to.

It isn't going to happen.

Ever.

Not like we wanted it to happen.

Not like we hoped it would.

Not like we thought it could.

And I know it now.

And I know there's nothing I can do.

Which is why I'm crying.

And laughing.

Because there's nothing funny about it.

"Radio?" says Mark.

"That'd be nice," I tell him.

"For what it's worth," he says, "Michael really loves you, Jessie."

I tell him, "Thank you."

And I lift my hands up to my eyes to hide my tears.

"Sure know how to cheer a girl up, don't I?" says Mark.

I say nothing.

"Years of practice," he says.

Sixty–eight

I wish it was raining.

I wish it was raining and chilly, so I could put on a warm sweater and build a fire in the fireplace and curl up in an overstuffed chair with a cup of hot cocoa and a good book.

That'd be nice.

Especially if it kept up.

The rain.

For about forty days and forty nights.

And if, when it was over, the Past was all washed away, and all that was left was the Present and the Future.

But it isn't raining, of course.

It's a bright, sunshiny day.

It's beautiful, damn it!

And I've got all this Past on my hands!

I've got all this unwashed-away Past to deal with!

Like Caroline—

Who I said I'd call and tell how everything went last night.

Except I don't want to call her and tell her how everything went last night.

Because I'm afraid everything went last night.

Meaning, Michael.

And me.

And us.

And what we've had together.

Like Michael—

Who said he'd be coming to see me today.

And who's supposed to be on his way here now.

He called after lunch.

It was after lunch for me.

For Michael, it was before breakfast.

He just woke up.

He wasn't sure exactly where, yet.

But he knew exactly where he was headed, once he got himself together.

First, to me.

And then, straight up in the air.

"Yeah," he said. "It went great last night—the show, Weinrib, everything! Wait 'till I tell you!"

Which I said I would.

And I have.

Ever since.

It's been about two and a half hours now.

I've been sitting out here—out in the bright, sunshiny day—perched on the fender of Lois's car, waiting for Michael's wagon to pop through the trees and glide into the clearing and come to a stop right across from where I'm sitting.

I've been sitting out here and I've been thinking.

Maybe I'm wrong!

I mean, last night it seemed real clear to me.

It seemed like I could never fit into Michael's world.

It seemed like Michael could never fit into my world.

297

In fact, last night, it seemed amazing that our two worlds had ever come together at all.

Or that they'd come together long enough for us to fall in love.

Long enough for us to be lovers.

And last night, it seemed real clear to me that our two worlds had only touched for a moment, and now—however much Michael and I might love each other—Michael's world and my world were drifting apart and taking each of us on our separate ways.

It seemed real clear to me, last night.

So how come it doesn't seem so clear to me now?

I mean, sure, I felt out of place with Jojo and Sandy and Red and Phyllis and everything.

Including Michael's new songs.

And what they're about.

And how he did them.

And how people reacted to them.

And how they reacted to Michael.

But maybe that's just because so much of what was happening was so new to me.

I mean, maybe I could get to feel *in* place with all that.

If I tried.

I mean, if I love Michael and Michael loves me, why should we let a little thing like our not feeling at home in each other's worlds get in our way?

Right?

Wrong?

Confused?

You bet.

And here he comes!

Perfect!

Here comes Michael, popping through the trees and out into the clearing.

Here comes Michael, and here goes everything!

Michael pulls his wagon up, right across from where I'm sitting, next to Lois's car.

Smiling through his open window at me, he says, "Did I mention that I love you? Last night? Did I?"

I smile over at him and hop down from Lois's fender.

I walk over to Michael and lean in through his open window and kiss him.

"Every way you could," I tell him.

He smiles.

"Go for a ride?" he asks me.

"Don't you want to get out and stretch?" I ask him.

He looks over at the cottage and then back to me.

He shakes his head and says, "No."

"I have to get back for dinner," I tell him.

"I've gotta be goin', too," he says.

It's not the answer I was expecting.

But then, I don't know what I was expecting.

Or what I am expecting.

Or what it is I want.

"Okay," I tell Michael.

I nod my head and start moving round to the passenger side of the car.

"Don't you want to tell your parents?" he calls to me.

"They're out in the boat," I answer. "Fishing."

He slides across the seat and opens the door for me.

"For dinner?" he smiles.

"Yeah," I tell him, hopping into the car and closing the door and taking a good close look at Michael's eyes, loving me.

"They could be a while," I say.

Moving closer, his eyes on mine, Michael shakes his head and says, "I wish *I* could."

And he kisses me.

It's not a long kiss.

But it's a loving kiss.

And a hungry kiss, too.

In fact, it's so deep and so quick, it takes me a second before I realize it's over.

I open my eyes to Michael's eyes.

Looking at me.

Loving me.

Hungering for me.

He smiles and slides back across the seat, behind the wheel.

He puts the wagon in reverse and backs around and drives us out onto the highway.

He doesn't say anything for a while.

And I don't, either.

Maybe he's thinking about what he wants to say.

Maybe he doesn't know, either.

Maybe he thought it was over last night, too.

Maybe he's not so sure today, either.

Maybe, maybe, maybe.

At least, there's music on the radio and pretty scenery out the window as we drive along the lake.

Finally—after we've been riding for five or ten minutes, I guess—Michael picks out a little wooded spot on the side of the road, a spot that looks out over the lake.

He pulls off the road and into this spot.

We have it all to ourselves.

Michael turns off the wagon and switches off the radio.

And we kiss, again.

Like before.

Not long, but longer than before.

Deeper but not quicker.

And we talk.

We talk a long time.

About last night.

And even though I was there, Michael tells it to me like a story, starting from the beginning—when Michael and the band pulled up to Fat City and climbed down out of their bus—and going through to when I left them in the dressing room.

And then, Michael breaks the story off and starts asking me what I thought of it.

How I felt about the crowd.

And the band.

And Michael's new songs.

And Michael.

But the thing is, all the talk—Michael's story about last night and the questions he's asking me—it's all parked-car talk.

Not because we're in a parked car.

Which we happen to be.

But because all the time we're talking, the expression on Michael's face tells me he's off somewhere, a million miles away, and nothing we're talking about here and now really matters.

But it does really matter.

It really matters to me.

Maybe not exactly what we're talking about.

But exactly what we're *not* talking about.

Meaning us.

Michael and me.

Where we are.

Where we're going.

If anywhere.

That's what we should be talking about.

Even though it scares me to death to even think about.

That's what we need to talk about.

I do.

But as long as Michael's talking parked-car talk, we'll never get around to talking about what I need to talk about.

Unless—

We might get around to talking about what I need to talk about if I could find a short-cut through Michael's parked-car talk.

If, for example, I could get him to jump to the end of his story, the part he's been saving to tell me last, the part about what happened last night, after I left Fat City.

"What happened?"

"Huh?"

I've interrupted Michael—asking me what I thought about the lights for last night's show.

"With Weinrib," I say.

"Oh," he says.

And the smile he's been wearing since he first pulled up to the cottage falls from his face.

"Bad news?" I ask him.

"Not exactly," he says. "More half and half. Like always."

"Always?"

"Ever hear of Wyatt Kiley?" he says.

"I don't think so," I tell him. "Who is he?"

He laughs.

"They're a band that had a Top Ten single last winter," he says. "'Kiddin' Who?' Remember?"

"Yeah," I tell him. "Why?"

"They're real good," he says. "Carlton Jeffries, Larry Suba—

"Michael!"

"They lost Randy Warden," he says. "He had a private plane he flew. He crashed it into a mountain."

"I'm sorry," I tell him.

"He was their lead singer and guitar."

"Michael—?"

He looks over at me from behind the wheel, a small sad smile playing over his lips, his expression a mixture of pride and pain.

"I am, now," he says.

I don't get it.

And I guess I must look like I don't get it.

"I'm the lead singer and lead guitar with Wyatt Kiley," he says.

"You're—?"

He nods his head.

"As soon as I get to L.A.," he says.

"Weinrib—?"

"Owns them," he smiles.

"And you?" I ask him.

He drops his eyes and slumps back against the seat, sighing deeply and shaking his head.

"What about the band?" I ask him. "Mark? Arnie? Emily? Leroy? Lenny?"

He looks at me—like a guilty but helpless little kid, asking to be forgiven.

"It didn't work out this time," he says. "Maybe next time."

I look away from him.

"Jess," he says. "Please, honey."

I look back.

He's right beside me.

"It's about the hardest thing I ever had to do," he says. "I need you to understand. I need you, Jess. With all my heart, I do."

And, leaning over, he takes me in his arms and kisses me.

I close my eyes—

Kissing him back—

Feeling everything—

How much I love him—

How much I want him—

And I promise myself, I'll remember everything—

Everything I feel—

Everything I've felt—

And I open my eyes.

And I push Michael away from me.

"It didn't work out this time," I tell him. "Maybe next time."

He just looks at me for a second.

And then he smiles.

And then he laughs.

A short, sad little laugh.

A laugh good-bye.

Sixty–nine

Fish!

I don't believe it!

When I get back to the cottage—

When Michael drops me off and drives away—

Bob and Lois are waiting with fish!

They are standing in the yard with these fish that they caught in the lake!

And Esther.

The whole scene reminds me of an ancient Russian proverb that I make up, right on the spot—

"Lose a lover, find a fish!"

"Fish!" shouts Bob, greeting me.

"Look!" shouts Lois.

"Look!" shouts Esther. "Fish!"

"Hey!" I say, joining them. "Fish!"

"Wasn't that Michael?" asks Lois, looking off toward the dust that's still settling in the clearing.

"Yeah," I tell her.

"Where's he going?" asks Bob.

"California," I say.

"Oh!" says Esther, impressed.

"For how long?" Bob asks.

"The rest of my life," I tell him.

"Oh, Jessie!" says Lois. "Would you like me to—?" She sees me shaking my head.

"To butt out?" she finishes.

"I'd appreciate it," I tell her.

Then, I turn away and start heading off toward the cottage.

"Where are you going?" asks Bob.

"I thought I'd go up to my room and cry until the fish are ready," I tell him.

As I arrive at the cottage, Bob calls to me.

"Are you serious?" he says. "About the fish?"

"No," I tell him, fighting back my sobs until I make it through the door. "We're just good friends."

Seventy

"When you didn't call this morning, I thought maybe it was because you were out so late last night, having a good time, and everything.

"But then—when you didn't call this afternoon—I started worrying that maybe you didn't have such a good time last night and that's why you probably didn't want to talk to anybody about it. So that's why I didn't call you," says Caroline.

It's nine o'clock that same night, and she's explaining why she's called me.

"But then—when it got to be after dinner—and you still hadn't called," she says, "I thought if you did have a problem, I should call you.

"So, do you?" she says.

If I didn't hurt too much to laugh, right now, I swear I would.

"I'm glad you called," I tell Caroline. "Michael and I broke up."

"Oh, no!" she cries.

"For good," I tell her.

"Oh, Jessie!" she says. "How awful!"

And she starts to cry.

Caroline starts to cry!

I can hear her.

And hearing her, I start to cry!

Again.

"Hey!" I yell at her. "Cut it out, will you? I'm the one who's supposed to be crying!"

"You are!" she yells at me.

"I am not!" I tell her.

"Are, too!"

"Am not!"

She starts giggling.

Caroline.

And—like it's follow the leader—I start giggling, too.

"Oh, Jess!" she laughs. "You must be crushed!"

"I am!" I laugh.

And she laughs.

And I stop.

And she stops, too.

"Do you want to talk about it?" she asks me.

"Not very much," I tell her.

"Any?" she asks.

"Well," I tell her, surrendering with a sigh, "maybe a little."

"What happened?" she asks. "Why'd you break up?"

Which—since it's the million-dollar question—cracks me up all over again.

"It isn't funny," she reminds me.

"*You* are," I tell her.

"Maybe," she concedes. "But what happened, anyway?"

"I think we got to know each other too well," I tell her.

"Is that a joke?"

"I wish," I tell her.

"If it's a joke, I don't get it," she says.

"I hope you never do," I tell her.

"Look, Jessie," she says, "you don't have to tell me what happened, if you don't feel like it. Just tell me."

"Michael's moving to Los Angeles," I tell her. "He's going to be a rock star."

"What?"

Seventy—one

It's around Christmas, the first time I hear it.

It's late in the afternoon, after school, and I'm going somewhere with Lois.

The two of us are just driving along in Lois's car, jabbering about something or other of major importance that I can't quite remember now.

And neither one of us is paying that much attention, when the guy on the radio says, ". . . our pleasure to introduce the new Wyatt Kiley. So let's give a listen—"

"Mom!"

"What?"

"Michael!" I tell her, zooming up the volume.

"Mi—?"

"Shh . . ." I tell her.

And I close my eyes.

And I lean back.

And there he is.

Michael.

Singing on the radio.

"Such a pretty song," I think. "So pretty and sad and str—my birthday song!"

Come Friday night, it's Alice.
Come Saturday, it's Sue.
I take my good times where I can.
The way most people do.
And Sunday night, it's Mary.
And Monday, Mary Lou.
And why I'll never love again
Has something to do with you.

It's such a sad song.
And so pretty.
I want to laugh, I'm so happy.
And cry, I'm so sad.
But it sounds real good to me.
My birthday song.
The first time I hear it.
All the way through.
It sounds wonderful, to be honest.
Like it's a hit.
Like Michael's a star.
"So near and yet so far!" I think.
And then, I open my eyes and look over at Lois, who's looking at me and waiting to hear my reaction.
I shrug and tell her, "Fair."
She shrugs and says, "Yeah."
Then, we both look out the windshield at the road ahead of us.
And break into laughter.

BRUCE AND CAROLE HART began writing for television in the late 1960s. They wrote some of the first scripts and songs for "Sesame Street" and also helped put together the Marlo Thomas special, "Free To Be . . . You And Me." They produced, directed, and—with Stephen Lawrence —wrote the songs for the television-movie "Sooner or Later," which was also their first novel. They also created and produced NBC's Emmy-winning series, "Hot Hero Sandwich."

The Harts write for young adults because they feel that "very few authors, filmmakers, television producers, etc. communicate honestly with young people about the important issues in their lives. Too often, this leaves young people feeling isolated, nonexistent, unimportant. It leaves them without a realistic perspective for dealing with their problems. We write to tell them that they are not alone and that what they care about matters very much—to them and to all of us."

Avon Flare Romance Novels

THE GIRL OF HIS DREAMS   **70599-0/$2.95 US/**
Harry Mazer   **$3.95 Can**
Sophie was not part of Willis's fantasy—neither the girl he imagined
for him nor in his plans for the big race—but their romance is a story
dreams are made of.

I LOVE YOU, STUPID! Harry Mazer   **61432-4/$2.95 US/**
                                                $3.50 Can
Marcus Rosenbloom, an irresistible high school senior whose main
problem is being a virgin, learns that neither sex nor friendship—is
ever very simple.

HEY KID! DOES SHE LOVE ME?   **70025-5/$2.95 US**
Harry Mazer   **$3.50 Can**
Jeff Orloff is ready to put his career dreams on hold for a chance at
the greatest love of all time. But what he can't understand is how a
world-class love like his cannot be enough.

RECKLESS Jeanette Mines   **83717-X/$2.95 US/$3.50 Can**
Fourteen-year-old Jeannie Tanger discovers the pain and bitter-
sweetness of first love when her romance with school troublemaker
Sam Bensen alienates her from her friends and family.

SOONER OR LATER   **42978-0/$2.95 US/$3.75 Can**
Bruce and Carole Hart
When 13-year-old Jessie falls for Michael Skye, the handsome,
17-year-old leader of The Skye Band, she's sure he'll never be
interested in her if he knows her true age.

WAITING GAMES   **79012-2/$2.95 US/$3.75 Can**
Bruce and Carole Hart
Although Jessie loves Michael more than ever, he wants more from
her. Jessie must make a decision. How much is she willing to share
with Michael—the man she's sure she'll love forever?